THE BURDEN IS LIGHT

Books by Eugenia Price

Eugenia Price

THE BURDEN IS LIGHT

The Autobiography of a Transformed Pagan
Who Took God at His Word
REVISED AND UPDATED

The Dial Press
New York

Published by
The Dial Press
1 Dag Hammarskjold Plaza
New York, New York 10017

Copyright © 1955, 1975 by Eugenia Price
All rights reserved.
Manufactured in the United States of America
First printing

Library of Congress Cataloging in Publication Data

Price, Eugenia.
    The burden is light.

    1. Price, Eugenia.   2. Converts—United
States—Biography.   I. Title.
BV4935.P75A32   1982   248.2′46′0924 [B] 81-17238
ISBN 0-385-27618-4   AACR2

TO

The One Who Dared to Call
His Burden Light!

Contents

Introduction

By Ellen Riley Urquhart

There still are some people in the world who believe the age of miracles is past. My observation is simply that these people have not met the author of this book. Her life has been one continuous miracle for almost five years, and I have watched it. In August of 1949 she was a tired, bored, radio writer with no belief in God. Six weeks later she was a relaxed, radiant child of God! The miracle in *her* life started in *my* life three years before and this is the way it began.

One day in New York City I wandered into a great church which was always open. I had hit an impasse in my life. In the face of an overwhelming circumstance my Christianity had collapsed. I was seeking to know why my Christian life seemed to fall to pieces every time I had something difficult to face. I hoped to find my answer in the silence of that great church. People came and went and I stayed on. Still groping for an answer, I walked up the long center aisle to leave the church.

A little old man with white hair and a lighted face came up another aisle. He was leaving, too, and we neared the door together. Quite suddenly he said to me:

"I beg your pardon. I am not in the habit of speaking to people I don't know, but the Lord has told me to tell you something."

We both stopped and he had the merriest eyes I have ever seen.

"I have a message for you, young lady. 'Seek ye first the Kingdom of God and His righteousness and all these things shall be added unto you.' " Then he repeated it and told me again that he did not make a point of stopping strangers.

Outside I was completely unaware of New York. My mind was fastened to the little man's message because I knew God had sent me a direct personal answer!

The key was in the word *first*. It made me see the root of my trouble. I was seeking a *victorious life* first but *I* was running my life. The Lord had just said to me, "Seek *Me* first. Let Me run your life."

This was completely clear to me that day, but it was several months before I was ready to put Christ first. When I did so, with no reservations, *everything* took on another meaning. I was no longer in the world to "be"—I was here to "belong." That changed everything. I began to get a deep insight into the words of Jesus: "If a man compel you to go a mile, go with him twain"; "He that saveth his life shall lose it"; "Whosoever shall smite thee on thy right cheek, turn to him the other also." I discovered that the ground is level at the foot of the Cross, and if we really follow Him we have to come along with the penitent thief who went with Him into Heaven.

This spiritual insight was the Lord's gift and it prepared me to meet Genie Price. Eighteen years had passed since we rollicked through our teens together and I hadn't seen her in all that time. But when I did see her again it was the right time because I had begun to take Jesus Christ at His word.

For a few days in the summer of 1949 we were both in our hometown of Charleston, West Virginia—she from Chicago and I from New York. When she called and asked me to be her houseguest, I was glad to go. But, more than that, while we were talking on the telephone something seemed to say, "This is important."

I remembered Genie as a pretty, happy-go-lucky girl who thought she owned the world. Standing beside me in her mother's living· room that day was a tense woman who was still desperately trying to *tell* herself that she owned the world. I knew that she was tired to death of the telling but she didn't dare stop. Her face looked as though she were warding off a blow. She might have called it "veneer." Magazine writers might have called it "sophistication." But the expression in her eyes was one I can never describe, and I felt somehow that she was at the end of her rope. Still, I was sure she didn't know *that* at all. A sense of urgency and destiny hit me. Although I saw tragedy on her face, at the same time I saw the possibility of a tremendous miracle, too. I knew that I was standing before "something" which from the human standpoint seemed very unlikely. Yet she was there as she was, and He was there as He is, and I knew the Shepherd had already laid down His life for the sheep.

While she was showing me over the new house her parents had built, my mind was trying to adjust itself to all the thoughts whirling there. She told me afterward that I didn't seem to notice the beautiful house very much. I was trying to admire it but my heart kept asking, "What *could* have happened to have made her this way?"

*

Genie will begin on the next page to tell in her own words what had happened before and what has happened since. My part in this book is simply to be witness to this amazing transformation which He has allowed me to watch these last five years. Watching for me has meant the deep joy of a rare friendship, many tears, much laughter, and a closer look at the face of Jesus Christ.

Part One

———— �֍ ————

B.C.

1

The First Time

I was born once and thirty-three years later I was born a second time. If this appears to be fantasy to you, read on and you will see that it is fact. And especially Reality.

This book is not being written because I was born the first time but because of the absolute *fact* of my second birth. It is after that in my life when things warrant writing a book.

*

Five years after I was born the first time (in Charleston, West Virginia, on June 22, 1916) I began the first grade one year ahead of time because I.Q. tests had become popular. Then excited teachers told my mother that I should "skip" grades. And Mother, being very young and also president of the Parent-Teachers Association at Elk School, said "all right."

I skipped 2-B, 4-B, and 5-A.

And in several years at three universities I never learned how to do the things in arithmetic which I had "skipped." I believe this is one of the ways I first learned the art of bluffing—which art I continued to cultivate until my second birth in 1949.

During my childhood we had very nice homes in which to live. We were completely average in that the more money my father made at his dental practice, the bigger and nicer homes we built. Mother always told me not to boast about it, but I did. I shared the basic insecurity of every American born to moderate means in a rich country. Early I caught the foolish belief that the normal thing to do is to move ahead materially. And then move ahead again.

And again.

We "built" according to this basic insecurity and felt perfectly honest when we said: "Oh, Grandmother wants to live on the river again and so we're building on the boulevard," or "The schools are so much better in this neighborhood," or "Since they widened the boulevard the traffic is unbearable."

I was rightly reminded that I sprang from good middle-class German, Scotch, and Welsh ancestors, that our new homes were just because Daddy was doing so well, and that I mustn't brag about it to the other schoolchildren.

But I did brag and was still doing it along all lines until I was born the second time when I was thirty-three years old.

Until I was *sure* for the first time in my life.

First I was born in a big white Victorian house at 1313 Bigley Avenue.

Then we "built."

The house we "built" was a large, then fashionable, brown bungalow right next door at 1311 Bigley Avenue. When I was about ten and very convinced that my father was undoubtedly the only really *good* dentist in the entire capital city of Charleston, West Virginia, we "built" again.

This time it was a big (then-fashionable) colonial house on the lot right next door to the no longer fashionable, brown bungalow.

Because I was her pet along with my father, my lunches were almost always prepared for me by my paternal grandmother, Callie Price, whom I called Gram. Gram was my mother's mother-in-law, my father's boss, and my champion. I know dear old Callie is rejoicing around Heaven as I write these lines because she did walk with God and only turned aside to storm up and down the peony bed now and then in a fit of "Stoffel temper." Gram had been a "Stoffel" before she married my well-loved country squire grandfather, Joe Price. And although Dr. E. J. Westfall preached the "complete cleansing" at Central Methodist Church, many people still did not quite believe that Christians do not *need* to lose their tempers! More accurately, that Christians *can* completely *lose* their tempers if they want to.

Grandmother Davidson was my mother's mother and we always called her Big Grandma because she was literally five by five and gentle and refined and mild and loved to put on a dark dress with a lace collar and have her picture taken.

Big Grandma and Gram got along because Big Grandma had such a sweet disposition, although she was not really converted to Christ until several years after I was born the first time. And the Sunday she received Him as her own, she really received Him as her very own and reached up with her pretty little plump hands and took off the two expensive purple plumes from her black velour hat.

This act characterized Big Grandma who married Bonnie Charlie Davidson, a self-styled psychiatrist from Scotland who admired himself very much and died and had his picture put on his tombstone when I was in 4-A. What I remember about him is that he was very handsome and didn't like the shape of various of his grandchildren's heads and predicted those children would come to no good end. He liked my head though and a few times he went on picnics with us and quoted Bobbie Burns and Keats to me while we sat under a tree and ate cold green beans, tomatoes, and corn bread—all three of which we both loved.

My country squire grandfather, whose name was Eli Edward Price but who was always called "Uncle Joe," caused one of my few childhood heartaches by dying before I was born the first time. Everything I had ever heard about him makes me long for the day when I will meet him in person when I, too, die physically. He owned the big general store and lived in a white house with a porch upstairs as well as down, in a town which spreads out along Elk River a few miles from Charleston.

"Uncle Joe" loved my pretty mother, Ann, whom Dad brought to live at the big Victorian house at 1313 Bigley after his parents moved into the city. During the days before "Uncle Joe" died, Mother spent long hours with him reading to him from the New Testament. Mother was so interested in the New Testament because she had just become a Christian shortly after she married Dad. They were converted together one night and Mother was very excited about Christ.

My father would be the first to agree that although he "went forward" with Mother and was "converted," religion was the property of Mother and Gram who didn't have too much in common with each other except religion.

I was like my Dad in almost every way and religion was definitely not in my department. I went to church because all "nice girls" did. Even though I hated being a "nice girl," as long as Mother let me wear high-topped boots with a pocketknife on the side and tomboy skirts with hip-pockets, ride my bicycle to school, and put on knickers the minute I got home, I agreed to "nice girl" dresses and suffered through Sunday school and church on Sunday mornings.

I didn't mind church too much because Mother conducted the choir; she was so pretty in her white robe with her beautiful auburn hair and her hands made such nice patterns as she led the good people through choruses and codas which should have been a little further out of their reach.

But I don't remember anything I ever heard in a sermon.

Dad and Joe and I sat and drew pictures and tried to make Mother laugh in the front row of the choir.

My brother Joe and I have to this day the kind of friendship and love that is rare because it has no strings on it. If this is a virtue on the part of either of us, it must be his because I bit his little finger and hit him on the head with a cologne bottle when he was a fat, pink infant in his crib. Mother vows I thought his finger was candy and that I was only experimenting when I hit him with the bottle. Mother and Gram always insisted that I was never in the least "jealous of the new baby."

Mother is beginning to see me now as I really am. Neither worm nor wonder, but "a bundle of possibilities in Jesus Christ." And this is setting me free in a way I was never free because Mother's approval motivated my life. And when I didn't deserve it, I found a way to get it anyway. I worshiped her and although I did exactly as I pleased when I was not with her, I would go to any lengths to keep her admiration and approval. My lovely mother was a Christian in my childhood, as deep a Christian as was likely, considering that by nature she is a very self-sufficient woman and was caught up early in the snare of "Christian service." And in an effort to "bring me up properly" she innocently added to my growing conviction that Jesus Christ was someone with a black beard who was out to spoil my fun.

The relationship that exists between my father and his only daughter is one that began in the mind of God even before little Walter Wesley Price was born to Callie and Eli Edward Price some sixty years ago. We had never had to work on our love for each other because we are as nearly alike as two people could be and still be two people.

Dad and I will never need to be reminded that we are sinners saved by Grace. We know it. And although He has captured us both now, I'm sure Dad had trouble, as I did, trying to conceive Jesus Christ. It was because of Him that Mother always had to "go to the church." He was distant and remote and yet trapped right there in the big stained glass windows. In one window He knelt beside a big rock and in the other He had a lamb in one arm and a big shepherd's crook in the other hand, and His face looked different in each window. I believe my Dad, like me, was unable to get Him to be one Person.

He was supposed to be a God of Love, and yet Gram walked hard through the upstairs hall so that things rattled when we didn't want to go to Sunday school to learn about Him. He was supposed to make people good and kind, but when I went to the church on Thursdays with Gram and played around the window seats of the Ladies' Aid Room where they quilted, I heard some of the members giving others what they called a "*good* tongue-lashing."

Once one of them got very red in the face as she shook her fist over the quilt and said she'd "never let a man inside her living room if he were smoking a cigarette even if it were the dead of winter and he were freezing to death!"

This did not seem very kind to me and I certainly did make every effort to hide my cigarettes from Gram and all her friends when I began to smoke at about fourteen.

*

I did not have very many close friends as I grew up because the Prices always prided themselves on being a complete family not in need of outside friends. But when I was very small a girl named Clara Alice lived next door in my grandmother's house where I was born, and we played together nearly every day. I was always told that I was calm and contained and poised, even though I bit my fingernails, and so I was simply fascinated with Clara Alice because when the doctor came to stick the little wooden paddle down *her* throat she could kick and scream and throw what was called a "tantrum." We made rose-petal "gravy" from petals we pulled off Gram's prize roses and we ate the "gravy," petals and all. I remembered doing that when years later I used to try to re-awaken my tired tastebuds by putting gardenia petals in highballs; I ate the gardenia petals, too.

There were other chums in high school and the usual boyfriends who fed my rapidly growing ego. And then there was Irvin who played his fiddle just a shade better than I played mine and was sensitive and had pretty white teeth and wore a white linen suit in the summer and bought me Evening in Paris perfume. I was madly in love with him from thirteen to fifteen. I don't remember the details but they were deep with emotion. When I went to college, however, Irvin became "frightfully far out of my world" because he still believed in God and wanted to know Jesus Christ's will for his life.

The last time I remember seeing Irvin we went out in the country in our car to get some holly and pine branches for Mother to decorate the church—possibly the last time she ever helped decorate it because I was already a freshman in college and our church days were quickly numbered after that. Irvin tried to ask me some serious questions like what I was "getting from college" and why I had stopped believing in God. I laughed at him and told him I had grown beyond anything so infantile. I explained that in a course in Comparative Religion I had learned there were many other religions, that the church people were superstitious hillbillies.

That there was no God.

That if there was, "it" was just some kind of force or abstract power. That a God of Love would not let such horrible things happen as happen in the world.

I said my whole life was going to be spent in having a good time and building my own career. When he asked what career, I said I didn't know but it would be mine! I said this life was all I was absolutely sure about and I meant to have all I could *take* of it.

He said something about my responsibility to my fellow man and I laughed again and told him I didn't ask to be born.

We gathered the pine branches and found a little bit of holly without any berries and he drove me home.

I thought him overly emotional then. I know now why he had tears in his nice blue eyes when he drove away that day.

2

Ellen Riley

Sometime between the age of eleven and the age of thirteen I met a girl at church who had big green eyes that slanted a surprising way and naturally curly brown hair. This made me very sorry for her because I was going regularly to the beauty parlor and thoroughly enjoyed the "maturity" of the thing. Without either one of us knowing it at the time, this girl became my best friend. I imagine both of us might have said quite casually then that two other girls were our "best friends." We wouldn't remember their names now but we were strangely unaware of having begun any vital friendship with each other then. Like Topsy we just "growed" together. Her mother had died not long before I met her and this also gave her a depth which I admired very much. Somehow it made her seem older and sadness always attracted me and made me want to run and help.

My friend with the slanty eyes and naturally curly hair and the "depth" was the best pianist around. When someone asked me to play a solo on my fiddle at church I found that if she accompanied me everything always came out all right. I hated to count and so played by "inspiration" and somehow she could always manage to be "inspired" the same way, or at least she knew just when to drop out a handful of notes—usually they were the same ones I dropped out.

"My, but the girls do play well together."

People said that over and over, although they talked all the while we were playing. But they kept asking us and I certainly did always prefer to have her accompany me.

Her name was Ellen Riley and she was about the only other girl I thought as pretty as I was. I haven't asked her if she felt the same

10

about me, but we did consider ourselves of immense importance in many ways.

We met at just the right time and felt just the right way about each other to "begin" a lot of things together. We "began" experimenting with variously advertised cosmetics together. We "began" dating at about the same time. We "began" making fun of people together. And when we played, as we did for about two or three years, for the annual revival meetings at the church, we "began" early to let everyone know that we played only because we were so sought after and we left immediately so no one could possibly think we had "gone religious." We "began" to smoke together also.

Ellen was born the first time one year before I was born the first time and that gave her an added "depth" to me. She had "skipped" the same number of grades in school and so gained still more stature in my sight because she was graduated from high school one year before me. We considered ourselves superior on every count, when we happened to pause long enough to do any type of considering. And through the years when we had completely lost track of each other I remembered "pointers" she had given me.

Pointers like this.

On Sunday mornings we would slip down with a couple of girls to what was then called Charleston Street and sit in the back booth at "Shaker Sadds," and drink Cokes and jauntily share a package of Old Golds. Soon afterward I changed my brand to Camels. But Ellen taught me on Old Golds, and in a distant world, tired and bored and trying to find it all again, many times I thought of the girl with the slanty eyes and curly hair and depth; and I remembered how she used to declare on Sunday morning in the back booth at Shaker Sadds (with all the maturity that a fifteen-year-old sophisticate could muster) that women should always hold a cigarette "up and away from their faces and never, simply *never,* flick ashes by beating on the top of the cigarette with the forefinger, but by gently touching same with a casually bent pinkie."

She does not remember these lessons. But she knows that I cannot tell a lie now.

And I remember them.

Ellen pursued a career in piano after high school and I went on to college. For no reason our paths separated, as paths do, for eighteen years. But I was *forced* to remember her now and then through the years in a way which I cannot explain but which I can simply describe, as I intend to do a bit later on.

3

Bridge

This is something of the way things were until I graduated from Charleston High School in 1932. My grandmother who lived with us had been giving me fur coats and hundred-dollar bills through the years vainly attempting to induce me to stop biting my fingernails. She had just begun to try in her misguided but well-meaning way to make me stop smoking et cetera and to begin to act like a nice girl, when she died one day and then for over eighteen years the Prices did not go to church at all.

Some of the pressure to go to church was gone. Mother had a serious illness and I began to pull hard away from God. Some people had some misunderstandings and after the illness we never went back to church. Somehow it was easier to stay out, although I know Mother did not mean it to be that way at all.

*

By that time we had "built" again because big, square, so-called "Spanish" stuccos with red tile roofs had become fashionable. Ours was at 712 Columbia Boulevard (now Kanawha Boulevard) and definitely a much better neighborhood. And on the Kanawha River.

And pleasing Mother had very nearly become my god.

4

Higher Education

In 1932 I went to college because it was the thing for Dr. Price's daughter to do. Mother thought it would be nice if I became a kindergarten teacher. I didn't because I definitely did not like children. But temporarily, until I had a chance to look around, that's what I did the first year.

As I remember I made two A's, one B, dropped two courses completely, and got one "incomplete" for cutting so many classes.

Also after the course in Comparative Religion when the professor asked in effect: "Where do Christians get off thinking theirs is the only religion where there are so many others?" I decided I was an atheist.

I did not decide this completely, however, until in Chemistry I learned how to write the formula for a sunset with certain colors. Without bothering to remember that God also created the chemicals that made up the sunset, I went back to the dormitory and cried and then it was that I became an atheist.

Also in my Freshman year I decided that I was not the sorority type, although I carefully made sure I had received bids to all the top ones before I decided. I would spend my life seeking complete freedom from any kind of confinement!

I tasted home-brew then for the first time because it was still the Prohibition Era and discovered, too, that I could write rather good sonnets.

In my Sophomore year I changed my course to straight Liberal Arts with an English major. I would write.

This was the pseudo-Bohemian year in which I gained entrance to the National Honorary Writing Society called, if I remember correctly, the Quill Club. And the piece on which I was accepted for membership was a long opus entitled "An Ode to Convention" in which I once more declared my personal *freedom*.

I finished my Sophomore year with my usual brilliant marks and "incompletes" and felt definitely that I had "grown away" from the sham and shadow of intellectualism and "art" and agreed with Mother that my skirts were too long and my hair too severe and since my eyesight was perfect, I would not insist upon horn-rimmed glasses because I no longer cared whether or not I appeared to be "gifted." Science had my attention.

The next fall, in my Junior year, I changed courses again and with my very first real purpose began digging for enough pre-dental credits to enter dental school the next year. I figured I could be really free in a lucrative career like dentistry. Free and different. My Mother and Dad had "weathered" the shock of another decided change and were "in it" all the way with me. As they always were.

I made excellent grades the next year and piled up enough needed credits and good marks to counteract some of my previous scholastic inconsistencies and surprised everyone but Mother and Dad by being the only woman to be accepted at Northwestern Dental School in Chicago for entrance the following year. I entered, made honor grades for almost three years, grew bored, quit, and dove headlong into philosophy with a brief sojourn at the University of Chicago for "atmosphere."

5

Near Reality

This period in my life from about twenty-one to twenty-four skirted very near Reality. Temporarily I seemed to step quietly out of the rollicking hedonism into which I had flung myself after I quit dental school and really wanted peace and good study and creativity and a home that was a home. This I had on Cornell Avenue in Hyde Park in Chicago in the neighborhood of the University. And even after I wandered away from the confinement of the classroom I spent long hours in deep books about literature and life and writing.

At this time *writing* became my god.

From sonnets with rhyme schemes and Edna St. Vincent Millay candor, I sought a new music and seemed to find it. I wanted to write something which was of "now." Because, as I wrote in a lengthy "preface" to a never-published collection of the poems which sprang from this time: "Now is the middle and the middle is quite different from the first." (Speaking of the century.)

In this "preface" which will either make good sense or no sense to you I also wrote: "Many people do not think that poets teach. But poets particularly are teachers." I knew I could be a poet right at that minute, but I also knew I had nothing to teach. And very little to say. I wrote also that "the poetry of today is value-lost in immediacy. It is not poetry in the true sense of now. It is poetry of immediate things and before them. And poetry of now in its truest sense is poetry of contemporary things and I beyond them." I knew these things but I did not know what lay beyond them. I seemed to want to know and yet there seemed no way of knowing.

In the very next paragraph of this "preface" I wrote something heartbreaking and empty and very true: "The one and first problem is the poet himself. He must live poetically before he can write poetry.

16

Poetic living produces poems because of itself. It is the antecedent of all poems."

I wanted to live poetically, sanely, simply.

I longed for simplicity of life.

I wrote of it and longed for it. At twenty-three I sat long hours on the back porch on Cornell Avenue and looked at the Illinois Central tracks and my heart cried out for something certain and simple and sane. At twenty-three years of age I was sick to death of ornate living and too many adjectives per sentence!

Suddenly I broke all my Tschaikowsky and Rachmaninoff and Ravel recordings and bought quantities of Bach fugues and toccatas and albums of Beethoven string quartets and clean, relentless piano Boogie Woogie.

I longed to be geometric about things even though I had almost failed geometry twice. But in this period I was not consciously trying to be what I was.

I was in certain aspects ridiculous, and sometimes I knew it, but I had begun an honest search.

After three years of not finding, I left the South Side of Chicago with a flourish and an extra stipend from Dad and took an apartment back on my dear Near North Side where I had lived during my first years in Chicago. Philosophy and even my own poetry which did please me very much had turned to ashes in my hands and I wanted to be back where there were people but fewer children and noise that was not the Illinois Central Electric; where the bars were better and where there were old marble mantels and wood-burning fireplaces.

I wanted to be back where it was the Near North Side again. And familiar.

At home in Charleston, Mother and Dad didn't "build" again, but they did extensively remodel a Victorian mansion which had been moved up the Kanawha River on a barge at great expense to old Mrs. Dawley who built it in the Gay Nineties. *Life* magazine ran pictures of its trip up the river and the Valley watched and when Mrs. Dawley died my parents bought it.

I moved, too, in Chicago. Back to my beloved Near North Side.

6

A Little Fawn Bulldog

As soon as I was moved into my lovely sage green apartment with a warm tea-colored marble fireplace on East Superior Street Spunky arrived, even before the bed arrived.

Spunky was not the name I would have given her because she was to me a goddess and a baby and my best friend. And although she was known to be fiery when one least expected it, Spunky told practically nothing about her "wonder." But my Dad had bred her and someone who bought her for a week when she was a puppy gave her that name, and then returned her for no reason anyone ever knew about except that she was intended to be mine all the time. She had already learned to answer to the name Spunky by the time she traveled from Charleston to live on East Superior Street with me and so we had to let it go.

But "Spunky" soon turned to "Pinkle" except when I wanted her to obey me. Usually I obeyed her because she almost always knew best first. Sometimes she was called "Pud," too, and as long as I used the "voice" that belonged to her, she responded with concentrated, depthless, delighted, and very focused love.

Response was her genius.

And I needed her response very much.

She was a little, cobby, low-to-the-ground, unusually marked, fawn brindle English bulldog—a show specimen, but I cherished her freedom and respected her hatred of any but very familiar territory and so did not show her after she had "cleaned up" in the puppy class for Dad back in Charleston. I still have her little loving cup from that event. But Dad said she trembled and waited for the show to close, and it was her last and she was very glad. She and I knew how gorgeous she was anyway and we were all that really mattered very much to either of us.

Spunky and I lived together under very varying circumstances and loved each other for ten hectic, extravagant, eccentric, ambitious, periodically successful, occasionally frantic and completely Godless years.

It was in this ten-year period that I learned to write for radio and did. Daytime serials and nighttime free-lance shows and then my own production office for the last five years before I was born for the second time in 1949.

I did not daily address myself in the mirror as "one who is a sinner and living entirely for herself." I did not know that was the situation. I couldn't have known it because I had long ago decided there was no such thing as sin or God and that nothing *was* actually right or wrong. Thinking merely made it seem so. I had become so neurotic that I could not have seen the sin in my self-life had someone told me about it. I felt that my parents were fortunate to have such a talented daughter (because I didn't dare feel anything else) and kept right on writing them elaborate letters about vague shows which were always just about to make me a big success and thousands of dollars.

Mother and Dad kept on believing in me. Or if they wondered they did not let me know about it. Once when I had sent Mother a sheaf of the poems I wrote on Cornell Avenue she wrote back that I must never let anything get in the way of developing my writing talent.

I know how she meant that but I took it to cruel extremes as I did many things. Stepping on faces ceased to bother me at all. And yet I saw to it that the people whom I liked and needed thought I was generous, kind, loving, and outgoing. The others I shut out.

May I repeat, I did not tell myself these things about my selfish self in those days. Because I did not know them at all.

Spunky may have known them because she watched me so closely. She never achieved a fondness for the smell of alcohol and seemed at times to be pulling me off to bed when she thought it was time to quit. She knew about the deep longings which I had ceased to recognize and when a desperate thought lingered too long and tore at me as I mosied along the gray, lake-misted, "Gold-Coast" streets while Spunky had her dawn walk before we went to bed of a Sunday morning, she would know it. And more than once she would take her attention from little grassy spots and exposed tree roots and come and sit right down on the sidewalk and bat at me with her round fat front foot.

Once I sobbed out loud on the street at dawn and she ran back and sat down and grunted her hoarse little grunt that said, "I love you. Doesn't it matter that I love you?"

It did matter.

Other people loved me, too, but often in the press of a roomful of close friends, through the scream of our determined gaiety, would slip that longing that turned wordless and sometimes sobbed when Spunky and I took our walks together in the evening or at midnight or at dawn.

If anyone remembered to ask me I would have said and did say that I didn't believe in God or any life beyond this one. The world ended with the top of my own head. But once a year I remember I prayed a kind of prayer to some kind of God. This prayer-time always came in the spring when Spunky was finding those first ecstatic traces of "life" in the black, half-frozen earth.

I didn't address God by any name, but I prayed every spring that if He did happen to exist would He please let me keep my dog until another spring.

He let me keep her for ten years and then one night after we had played like rough children on the living room floor with some big boxes of recordings I was shipping out to radio stations the next day, Spunky looked at me and asked for help. She was too old then to jump up on my bed, and so she had begun to sleep on the floor on a big, soft alpaca blanket. I got down there beside her and held her while she cried her hoarse little cry.

I swore at the vet on the telephone when he said there was nothing we could do for her; that she was older than most bulldogs already. I felt vaguely sorry later when I remembered that I hung up on him in a wild fury of fear.

Didn't he know she was the most important thing in the world to me? He knew it. He loved her, too. He had saved her life twice. But in a few minutes she stretched out her little back legs like a frog the way pedigreed dogs often do, slipped out her pink tongue about an inch over her lower teeth the way bulldogs do when they sleep, sighed deeply, and left me.

I touched her eyeballs and she didn't blink. I called her in "her voice." But she couldn't wiggle her little curly feather tail anymore. She was dead.

She would have responded to me if she could have but she was dead.

I sat in the house with no reason to take walks any more and felt death in me, too. I bought another fine female bulldog named "Petunia," and she was a darling, but she was not Spunky. I was just not capable of another intense friendship, and so I gave her back to the people from whom I bought her in Indianapolis. And one day I sat alone on the front steps where I used to sit with Spunky and *almost* realized that nothing really mattered in my whole life enough to bother to write it down.

I didn't have anything coming up which I had to write and it was a good thing because I had nothing whatever to say.

7

Very Heavy

I had nothing whatever to say as a writer and so I dreamed up one or two formats for sports shows which would be built around boys and girls. They were designed for quick sales to beer and/or cigarette sponsors.

I had nothing whatever to say as a writer and I was very heavy. Not only was I at least sixty pounds overweight from so much sitting around cultivating gourmet eating and drinking tastes, but there was so much added "weight" around my heart.

Layers and layers of it. "Stone" it used to be called in Victorian verse and in 1920–30 popular song lyrics which implied that the person who had a "heart of stone" just did not care. I doubted this and found that I was right. If we do not care we do not bother to weep into quick rhyme-schemes and liquids aged in wood. The stone around and in my heart was not from *lack* of feeling. But from feeling too much and from being completely locked up in it.

I was heavy. Things were heavy for me. In spite of periodic financial success the debt grew heavier and the lies to the creditors grew in proportion to the debts. Naturally I blamed life and that added a heavy load of resentment. I had what I thought I always wanted and then didn't want it enough to accept the responsibility for it. I deceived my parents and one friend in particular. And I hated myself—heavily. But saw no way to change and so eventually dodged behind the thick (heavy) wall of neuroticism and declared more loudly than ever that I loved things just as they were.

Self-deception is very, very heavy.

Fear is very, very heavy.

Worry is very, very heavy.

It is heavier even than these when you have spent your life convincing

22

yourself and everyone else that you are a success and then have to be—or find a way out of it all. Money isn't exactly what you mean either, although you tell yourself it is.

Money bought another fine female bulldog when Spunky died, but she was not Spunky.

The heaviest thing of all is to have no beginning and no end.

No Alpha and no Omega.

No reason for waking up in the morning although so much of what you have always thought you wanted is all around you. A nice house, friends you love, your own office, your record collection, and the possibility of more of the same for all of your life. And all of your life was only about thirty-five or forty more years, so did it matter so much if you were so bored you looked at the food almost every time you sat down to eat and wondered why some palooka couldn't invent another vegetable?

Boredom is not smart. Boredom is very, very heavy.

I would never have used a word so Biblical as "burden" except in doggerel, but that was mostly because I might have cried with embarrassment or fear of facing things as they were.

And even though I would not have used the word, considering it obvious, things were—a *burden* to me.

All of life was a burden.

A very heavy burden.

8

The Burden of August, 1949

All of life was a burden and I was tired from carrying it myself. Tired and overweight and bored and afraid to admit that I was afraid. Able to convince myself for certain hours out of the twenty-four while under the influence and sway of the rhythms and madness and ecstasy of certain favorites from my fine collection of jazz music that life was like *that*. Mad and ecstatic and rhythmic. Or could be now and then and that would be enough. Along with books.

But outside of these times it was all heavy and more and more was required to stimulate or interest me. I was considered successful and I was thirty-three, but everything was heartbreakingly heavy.

Like this I went home in August of 1949. For some reason I remember that my pullman reservation was marked August twelfth. At home in the clean, newly built elegance of my parents' long, low, stone ranch house high on the top of the highest hill around Charleston, things looked better as they always did. And as always, when I came under Mother's influence I wanted to change myself. And as always I stopped drinking and went on a diet.

I didn't need to drink at home anyway. I could have and did occasionally, but we had fun at home and it was always for such a short time that I didn't have a chance to get restless. I became a child there, with no responsibility to escape.

As a result of my chaotic, self-centered inner life, I always left deep unhappiness behind me in Chicago but this time I had brought a heavy load of it home with me.

There wasn't any great catastrophe over which to gnash my teeth and dwell on in second-act-curtain finalities. There was just deep unhappiness lying there wondering at all the empty space around it.

And I sat on the patio outside Mother's kitchen door on the top of the hill and drank black, iced coffee because of the diet and smoked and tried not to think. I tried just to look at the height and depth and green of the top of the grove of ancient oak trees beneath which our home is nestled just before the grove moves down over a steep wooded ravine.

I was home again. As all the other years. It was summer. I liked myself sun-tanned and so set about getting a tan. Dad brought me suntan lotion and a couple of cartons of Camels the first night and we talked lots of baseball. I knew everyone's major league batting average then. Some of my inner unhappiness could have been caused by the Chicago Cubs and was. But "emptiness" was more to the point. Dad brought me suntan lotion and Camels and that week's issue of *Variety*, as he always did, and Mother asked me please to lose lots of weight and showed me her new bird books, and we decided the names of the birds that flocked in bright, quarreling dozens to the stone bench outside the windows where we ate breakfast. No one said anything more except how much fun it was to be home. And how glad we were that Charleston had its own Class A baseball club that year.

Mother looked at me now and then as though her heart would break and they both seemed to be trying to cheer me up.

On the diet I lost about nine pounds in five days since I always did everything extremely and then during the night of August seventeenth I had the dream again.

9

The Dream

Writers, particularly commercial writers, have many mountains that are quite high and many valleys that are quite low. Especially are there many valleys that are quite low.

Emotionally and financially.

At these "valley times" I would always go home and Mother would buy some new clothes designed to "do something" for the bulges we were continually battling, remind me of my great talent, tell me how much she loved me, how much she expected of me. Then they would give me a hundred dollars or so bonus for being their daughter and Dad would drive me to the station or the airport and then prepare to cheer Mother up after I had gone.

There was one other thing that happened at many of these low periods through the years. Over this I had no control. It was sub-conscious. It was a dream.

I cannot write pages of vital description because the dream was very simple. I was always the age I was while dreaming it. But the setting was an overgrown, tangled garden in which children were playing and laughing. Really laughing. Not the substitute which shrieked from the windows of my various apartments in Chicago. This was the kind of laughter I have found again when Christians are together and relax, remembering Christ is there, too.

In the midst of this laughter and play in the dream I would walk down a path at a certain time by my watch (the one I really wore) and there sitting under a happy old apple tree, would be Ellen Riley as she was when we were effervescing teen-agers. Nothing happened except Ellen always jumped to her feet (as fifteen-year-olds do) and exclaimed that she was so glad to see me back again.

I said she "always" did this because I suppose I must have had that same dream at least a dozen times in ten or fifteen years. Nothing ever stimulated me like that dream and its good effect lasted sometimes three or four hours.

It made me feel all clean inside and not a bit tired.

I didn't tell anyone about it. People in the world have one diagnosis: "Old girl, you're going at things too hard"—no matter what. So I didn't tell anyone. I would have felt silly. Having the same dream over and over. And such an innocent dream with no interesting overtones nor mysterious undertones.

Well, that was the dream I had again at home on August 17, 1949, when things were so heavy in my life everywhere I looked.

The new stone ranch house was beautiful and all the long expanse of picture windows made the oak trees come inside, but the debt on it was heavy, too. This was going to be an added burden to Dad who never complained but had stood beside his dental chair for thirty-eight years already.

Mother was a magnificent manager though and being the Prices we figured of course we'd make it.

I was annoyed that they hadn't borrowed ten thousand more dollars to put on a roof of hand-tied, wooden shingles, but the fifty-five foot combination living room and dining room definitely "did something for me" as I wandered back and forth through it during those August afternoons when Mother and Dad were downtown at the office. People had said I was really eccentric when I had the wood-paneled walls all stained a permanent, cool, forest green. For once I was right and this victory also "did something for me" as I walked up and down the fifty-five feet of glass and wood and stone and tried not to think anything in particular.

I did this for several days while I dieted and sat in the sun and then during the night of August seventeenth I had the dream about which I have just written.

10

A Telephone Call

Usually I slept until eleven both at home in Charleston and in Chicago but on the morning of August eighteenth I got up and had breakfast with Mother and Dad.

The sun was so bright I had to move to the extreme end of the long, glass-topped Italian iron table where we sat on the longer window-side of the huge kitchen. This annoyed me and made me feel all over again the heaviness I pulled out of bed with me that morning because I couldn't see the birds very well from that end of the table. And the birds lightened things.

As you know, I had had the dream before. And it had always picked me up. This time it was different. I was troubled and things felt heavier than ever. Even the coffee pot was heavy after Mother and Dad had gone to work and most of the coffee was gone. But before they left I asked Mother what ever happened to Ellen Riley.

It had been so long since I had inquired after anyone from Charleston that Mother was quite surprised but as usual didn't press me with questions. "I don't know, dear. Haven't seen her or heard of her in years. The last I did hear she won some sort of piano prize at White Sulphur Springs."

And then Mother said a most amazing thing which probably won't sound at all amazing. But considering the fact that she religiously respected my hatred of seeing anyone from home during my brief visits there over the years, it was almost amazing. I had just held my match for Dad to light his cigarette when Mother asked: "Why don't you call her today?"

I laughed first and said, "Please!" which implied, *"Please* make sense when you speak, woman. You know I don't want to dig into anything tired and gone. That was a high-school friendship and no doubt Ellen is married now and has umpteen children and is interested

28

only in them and is tired and stoop-shouldered from picking up after her husband all these years.''

I didn't say all of that but my ''Please'' said it for me. Mother and Dad had long since learned to fill in after that ''Please!'' They knew it always implied that I was somehow being imposed upon or going to be if someone didn't wake up and prevent it.

It is a frightening thing to fear boredom and unfamiliar surroundings and strangeness as I did. I didn't admit fear but it had long ago admitted me to its inner chamber and there held me captive by many chains—not one link of which I would or could recognize.

Mother suggested that I call Ellen and I poured another cup of coffee and said, ''Please!'' Dad and I talked about baseball for ten minutes and after they had gone to work I sat there alone feeling the weight of something I might have called ''cosmic'' and then I went to the telephone in my room and began trying to remember Ellen's aunt's name so I could look up the number.

I knew she used to live with her Aunt Addie on Indiana Avenue but I had to call Mother to find out her aunt's last name. Mother's voice was warm and helpful. Even more than usual. She said, ''Call and then let me know what's happened to Ellen after all these years.''

All these years were eighteen.

Aunt Addie answered but I just asked to speak with Ellen, please, as though I knew she'd be there still living with Aunt Addie. In a few seconds Ellen said, ''Hello.''

Becoming immediately brisk and sharp of diction as I always did, especially when speaking with someone from West Virginia who had not worked as I had done to lose the soft, flat vowels, I opened with:

''Hello, darling . . . this is Genie Price. Remember me?''

She said she certainly did and that she had been living in New York City for six years and that it was strange that I should call just at the time she was home on vacation.

For a minute I wanted to hang up and pretend I hadn't called at all. Then I heard myself selling Ellen on the idea of spending the weekend with me in my parents' ''lovely new hilltop home.''

In a quiet, definite, economical way which I have since learned to love and depend on and never question, she said: "All right. I'll come."

And she did—the next afternoon in a taxi. She wore a black linen suit which made her seem quieter than I remembered her; except for that and a suggestion of a coming-crinkling around her still slanty green eyes, she looked exactly as she looked when we were fifteen and sixteen! I exclaimed about that, of course, beause I always exclaimed about everything and she seemed very charming but kind of dazed and not with me at all.

I know why now.

She has told me since that at that moment when she stepped in the side door of our home and saw Genie Price looking as I looked she was rocked to the depths of her being. I had been a "bubbler" in the old days and very happy and very delighted about things of all kinds.

And then there I stood looking as I looked in August of 1949.

And she says now it was as though the Lord put His hand on her shoulder as we stood uncomfortably and very strange together just inside our living room door that day and said: "Ellen, this I want." She replied, "Oh, no, Lord—not that!"

But she loved me as we stood there and that was His doing, too.

Finally I took her overnight bag to my room and offered her a cigarette. She said, "No thank you," and smiled. I then took her on an elaborately conducted tour through our new home and wondered why she seemed so quiet about the whole splendid thing.

We sat down in the living room after a while and I asked her what she would like to drink. That was simple courtesy to me. And I needed one by then. Diet or no diet.

She smiled again and said she didn't drink. And added that she didn't because she didn't need to anymore.

This intrigued me but I let it go. And I let my drink go, too. For the next hour I stormed the conversation with highly exaggerated accounts of my great successes as a radio writer over the years including the promise to play as many recordings of various shows which I produced out of my own office as she was teeming to hear since I had had a special transcription playback made for Mother, et cetera, et cetera, et cetera, ad nauseam.

She listened quietly and at one point when my voice was way up and bragging she broke in: "That's all very interesting. I know you've done some fine work, but you're probably the unhappiest-looking person I've ever seen, Genie. What's really the matter?"

If you have ever heard your own defense shatter, remember that sickening silence that follows the crash right now and share it with me as I sat there with an unlighted cigarette in my hand afraid to look down at the wreckage around my feet.

She was not unkind. In fact, her expression and her voice were so kind I quickly lighted the cigarette and faked a cough while I batted away the tears that were there brimming.

After that I told her things which I had not even dared admit to myself. We were very close and yet we were shouting to each other from opposite shores of the universe.

The shore on which she sat was friendly and the trees waved and things grew.

The shore on which I sat was washed and barren and there weren't any trees at all and nothing wanted to grow.

Outside my lovely family home stood the oak trees that made the lot so expensive. There were no hilltop lots nor fifty-five-foot living rooms nor big dramatic productions in Ellen's life, but on the shore where she sat the tall trees clapped their hands and beckoned to me.

The universe backed up her life.

I was breaking myself over the laws God built into the same universe when He created *it* along with Ellen and along with me. She knew He created her and she knew that as long as she lived His Way the universe which He also created would back up her life.

And so we sat there shouting at each other from the opposite shores of the universe and the more I crumbled the more clearly I could hear the longing in my heart.

Those walls, behind which I had been hiding since I stopped being the wide-eyed, happy "bubbler" Ellen had known eighteen years before, were crumbling and I wanted to scream and run before the

Light broke through and showed me what I had become.

Ellen talked about what was at the center of her life. She said it hadn't always been that way. Just about three years, in fact. But she couldn't do some of the things I did because "they wouldn't fit with what is at the center of my life."

Of course, I walked right in and asked: "All right, *what is* at the center of your life?"

She said: "It isn't a 'what.' There's a Person there."

"A person?"

"Jesus Christ."

What did I reply?

"Please!"

That's what I said and laughed but I didn't feel at all like laughing. I laughed because I didn't know what else to do and certainly I didn't know what else to say.

11

The Cross

We played some Bach recordings and Ellen said she felt God in them. I laughed again and said I felt Bach in them and that was almost too terrific for me to bear at times.

Then we played some of my jazz records. Boogie, New Orleans and Kansas City. I reacted to these as lovers of true jazz react and Ellen sat and listened quietly and found one (a Julia Lee recording) whose melody was so simple and haunting she could say she loved that melody and mean it. She did and I was somehow very relieved.

I see now that she loved it because it was such a good description of all the wounds which need to be "answered by His wounds."

We talked to the family that evening and then we went to our end of the house and prepared to go to bed. Sitting on the side of my bed smoking one cigarette after another, I asked:

"What do you really believe about God?"

"I believe God came to earth in the Person of Jesus Christ to show us what He is really like. And to save us from sin."

"Sin!"

"Yes, sin is anything that separates us from God, and there isn't any way to get back to Him except by believing in Jesus Christ and what He did on the Cross for us. We just *have* to be forgiven."

I smashed out my cigarette.

"Cut that stuff about the Cross! That I won't listen to!" Then I lighted another cigarette, missed the ashtray when I threw the match at it and snapped:

"Don't insult my intelligence."

That was such a trite, obvious thing to have said that it proves my frightened confusion at that moment so that I feel I need say no more about it now.

Ellen said no more that night either. I sat there smoking for a long time and wished with all my heart that she hadn't dropped off to sleep.

*

A few chapters back I spoke of a group of poems I had written when I was about twenty-three and had almost found Reality. If you are one kind of person you will love these poems. And most especially if you are anything like Ellen you will understand them better than I understand them. If you are another kind of person you may not even think they are poems. That is all right. All I say is that they are mine. And that night after Ellen spoke of the Cross of Jesus Christ this one kept racing through my mind:

> Time is
> Hang-rope
> And snares
> The going-on.
> I must
> Walk faster
> And arrive
> At time
> Bent-back
> To meet
> The going-in!

I remembered it all even though I had written it some ten years before. I *was* "walking faster" without meaning to. I clung to control. Desperately.

"Sin is anything that separates us from God, and there isn't any way to get back to Him except by believing in Jesus Christ and what He did on the Cross for us. We just have to be forgiven!"

Why do we have to be forgiven?

I had never been able to memorize my poems and yet there was another one crowding in:

Another way
I am not I.

Pardon is
The gist

And 'yes'
Instead of

'No' and
Changes

Number-know
To see and

To begin
To be.

Ellen said "We just *have* to be forgiven!" My poem said: "Another way I am not I . . . *pardon* is the gist."
Forgiveness.

*

The next day was Sunday and Ellen acted as though she didn't notice that no one mentioned going to church anywhere. I must admit I was not even thoughtful enough to say no one would be driving off the hill that day.

We played more records and listened to the symphony in the afternoon and God was *everywhere* I turned! I hoped to move Him to the margin at least, by dragging out Mother's yellowed copies of the poems which had dodged in and out of my mind all night long.

This was also amazing because I had long since considered it extremely poor taste to show anything one had written to anyone outside of one's intimates. Or fellow writers. As poor taste as to offer to play the piano or to mention the price of your new living room rug.

But in order to get God out of the picture for a while so I could retain *my* familiar place in the *center* of things, I dragged out the poems.

Ellen read a little short one first. Then she read two more longer ones.

"You won't like this but the thing I find in your poetry is a big, wide God-hunger!"

I laughed.

She read another one and there were tears in her eyes. There were no remarks about the fact that I left out words and made free with verbs. My poems seemed natural to her! And she seemed natural with them. But the ones which amused me made her want to cry.

I was completely in the dark as to what she was really thinking, and at times even she seemed not to know. I thought she was embarrassed some of the time, but as I usually did in those days with her, I missed the point completely. I know now what she was doing when she sat for such a long, to me, nervous time without saying anything out loud so I could hear.

Then she looked at me as though this had never been true of anyone else at all before that time:

"Love is really important to you, isn't it?"

"No."

"I don't believe that."

I laughed and said: "Well, I can lie. I'm not a Christian."

"I think love is very important to you and absolute miracles could happen the day you begin to know Divine Love!"

Missing her point again, I said I no longer believed love without self-interest was possible.

Kahlil Gibran said it was, and I had meditated "profoundly" over *The Prophet* in my late teens, but it had dust on it now.

I had loved people. One or two I had loved very, very much. I loved my parents, but my behavior proved that I did not love anyone quite as much as I loved myself.

Ellen read more of my poems and I knew she understood them better than I had understood them because I did not mean to be writing about the things she read into them. One was titled "Peace

By One." She said, "Peace *is* only by One." I didn't think I meant
Him at all! She read them all and I just sat there trying to look only
vaguely interested and said nothing. She closed the notebook and
asked me a very strange question:

"Have you ever read 'The Hound of Heaven'? The poem by
Francis Thompson?"

"Yes. Back when we took English from Mary B. Jefferds in high
school. Why?"

"I just wondered. I like your thin, simple style much better than
Thompson's, but somehow I thought of 'The Hound of Heaven' just
now."

I knew the "Hound of Heaven" was Jesus Christ.

And God moved once more from the margin to the center of our
conversation. I doubt if He had really moved out of it. I believe He
caused me to recall the poems. I hadn't even looked at them for ten
years.

12

Incident

That evening Ellen sat down at Mother's new grand piano and played a composition entitled "Malagueña" which is not exactly spiritual in character but which is very, very showy. Long-haired musicians like Ellen play it and harmonica players make records of it. Its beat is Spanish and definite and primitive in spite of the flowery right hand. You probably know it and wonder why I am devoting a paragraph to "Malagueña" when she also played Chopin and Schumann and Bach. There are two reasons. One is her extreme skill in making it sound like much better music than it is. The other is that although it is definitely not spiritual, it will come up again and again in our story and I want you to recognize it when it does.

She played "Malagueña" and even my brother Joe, who is strictly anti-longhair, said: "Say, that moves!"

Later on that same evening after Joe went back to his own home and Dad had gone to bed with the sporting news, Mother suggested that we have some iced grape juice. It was August and West Virginia and very hot.

I prepared it and brought in three glasses on a tray. Ellen, who weighs exactly one hundred and two pounds, said she was still not hungry from dinner or even thirsty. For some strange reason this annoyed me. Probably because I weighed quite a bit more and was both hungry and thirsty and so I held the glass of grape juice straight out and said:

"Aw, come on, little saint. Take the sinner's grape juice. You can make like you're having Communion and you'll *love* it!"

Mother said: "Why, Genie!"

Ellen winced as she took the blow for Him and that was the first time I had seen pain on her face. Although I had tried to hurt her several times, this was the first time it showed.

13

The Plane

Ellen had to go back to her job in New York City in another week. Having run my own life for so long I was annoyed that she wouldn't write her employer or call long distance and say she was ill. I even offered to call for her. But she was firm in the quiet little way that only one hundred and two pounds of indwelling can be firm and after spending another night at our house later on in the week she went back to New York.

Actually, when she was so definite about not being able to lie to her employer I suddenly didn't even want her to come back to my home for the second visit. I swore to myself because I had even asked her. I had nothing in common with a religioso! What was my trouble? She seemed to sense this and made very sure that I didn't get a chance to back out on the invitation.

She knew she *had* to come again.

And then the next morning Mother and I stood on the back balcony of our house and waited for the big, silver four-motored plane to take off for New York City. From our hilltop, looking out and across the valley and the river to the top of the hills on the other side, we can watch the big planes take off from Charleston's unique hilltop airport. Her plane left on schedule and as it circled over our house and disappeared into the hot August sky it was as though before the takeoff someone had fastened a chain around my heart and hooked the other end to the big ship. The smaller it became on the horizon, the more the pain increased in my chest.

Ellen and I had so little in common except that she understood my poems as few had understood them, and I decided that must be the reason I felt that way because most people thought I was a little crazy after they read them. I had written them and put them away and then made money doing for radio what people called "fine writing." But she hadn't even thought the poems peculiar. She said they were new and clean and fresh.

And simple and clear and young.

I didn't feel any of those things as I watched the plane disappear from sight. But I wanted to cry because someone had thought that again about the poems. Instead I smiled what I hoped was casually at Mother and said:

"Ellen's turned into a real puzzle. She's so talented *and* attractive." And then I stretched and pretended to yawn. "Isn't it too bad she's gone religious? It will all be wasted now."

14

Letters

I stayed on in Charleston another week or so and then wandered back to Chicago. But during that week I could scarcely believe it when every day in the big green mailbox on the curly iron stand by the road at the front of our house there was a letter from her in the soon-to-be familiar southpaw penmanship. Some were just little notes. They spoke often of the poems and eased me in gradually on the nature of her work in one of the big New York churches and they told me little things that happened and always they moved straight into the center of my heart. While she was visiting me, I had talked so much about "my work" she had very little chance to tell me about hers.

Her letters never spoke of God unless I did in my reply. They never quoted Scripture because she knew I was very much against it. But the one I received just before I went back to Chicago said:

> Remember I did see another "you" begin to emerge, and I don't believe anything can stop "her" now. This new thing isn't something that you have. It is something that has you. Remember that, Genie, if you get low—especially after you go back to Chicago. I know so well that even now things will look different. Something has you and most likely you will not be able to forget. You'll have to face things back there and you don't know what your reaction will be, and you feel as if you don't really know yourself, I imagine. But when that happens get away by yourself and just stay there and be still and then remember the Something *which has you*. When you remember that you won't have to keep trying to "find it" as you say. I wish you would get alone every day. Do you think you could? I find myself wishing I could run ahead of you back to Chicago

and protect you from the bewilderment that will come, but you are the one who has to go back and you will know that I'm with you in it. And more than that, things will work out. This may sound crazy, but I feel this is only the beginning of Something so great I can't fathom it. I'll pray as you asked me to. I am now. I shall be always.

Love,
Ellen

Just before I left for Chicago another letter read in part:

The only kind of life you have *known* to live so far is bound to bring one crisis after another. That isn't criticism, Genie. That is just a law of the universe. And when the next crisis comes to you, remember I'll have the answer for it. You don't need to ask me to pray for you. It is as though Someone prays through me for you every minute. I am amazed at all this. I am in awe of it. I'll write again tomorrow.

I've never done this with you, but forgive me if I quote one little verse from the Bible? "And it shall come to pass, that before they call I will answer and while they are yet speaking I will hear."

Keep up the diet. I'm pulling for you.

Love,
Ellen

When I arrived in Chicago the letter that was waiting there said:

For some reason I feel you will be in New York soon. Am I completely crazy?

I thought she was and dismissed the idea. But, of course, she wasn't and of course the crisis came almost at once and instead of drinking as I fully intended to do, I got on a train for New York and started—thinking.

A close friend of mine handed me a book just before I got on that train to New York. It had been handed to her by someone whom she did not particularly like and who did not particularly like her. She hadn't read it, but just as though she were operating under Orders, she handed it to me. It was a book about an atheist who had become a Trappist monk. I wanted to forget that I had it, but I was *forced* to read just enough of it so that by the time the train was hurtling through Pennsylvania another horizon had been smashed!

I can't find the part in the book now and maybe it wasn't even anything I read. But all of a sudden I looked out the train window at the sky and *knew* life did not end here.

15

A Very Different New York

Ellen was on the staff of Calvary House which was next door to the old Calvary Protestant-Episcopal Church where she had come into her vital walk with Christ. When she was in her early twenties back home in Central Church, Ellen was converted through Dessie Arnett, her Sunday-school teacher. But after she went away from God for a time in New York she came back to Him to find Him altogether real. And Dr. Samuel Shoemaker who was then rector of Calvary Church and his wife, Helen, were among those who showed her Christ as He is. And so when I met her again after all those years her address was Calvary House, 61 Gramercy Park. Calvary House is a big comfortable eight-storied brick building where missionaries of all denominations stop on furlough and where people of all walks of life may live at reasonable rates and learn to walk with Christ as a living person. Ellen was hostess in the dining room at Calvary House.

Hating churches as I did I refused to stay there, so I ensconced myself in a large front room at the nearby Gramercy Park Hotel and called Ellen on the telephone.

This was on Monday right at the end of September during World Series time in 1949. For the first time in years I did not listen to the World Series at all. I was very busy with God. And since it "*is* a fearful thing to fall into the hands of the living God," what happened from that Monday until the following Monday morning when I got on another train going back to Chicago will have to be told in impressions. I don't remember it clearly in sequence.

A few definite things are that the room service was excellent in the hotel and a big steam shovel was excavating for something right across the corner and from my windows I could see the interiors of very well-turned-out apartments. One had a beautiful dark green wall.

For years in Chicago I had affected green walls—a certain sage green and people called my home "the Green Room" and came there and talked and were "brilliant and gay" as people are supposed to be in theater "Green Rooms." This one across Gramercy Park from my hotel room was a darker green and much more elegant. I remember the walls as being partly paneled. They may not be. It also looked quiet.

I called Ellen on the telephone as soon as I had dismissed the bellboy who brought up my luggage. I still had on my new brown velvet hat with a veil when she flew into the room a few minutes later very glad to see me. And very careful with me as I look back now.

I was still walking in darkness. I had not been made a new creature yet. But I had fallen into the hands of the living God and somehow I felt sure Ellen never really stopped praying even though she chatted gaily with me and tried to make plans for us to go here and there to nice French restaurants in the neighborhood until she saw that I was not interested at all in doing that. I had done it so much before. So had she. And just when she was saying we'd talk about all that later I blurted:

"I believe there is another life after this one."

"You do, Genie?"

"It came to me on the train. God only knows why it came, but it did. And I know there is now."

"That's wonderful." She looked as though she were listening to Someone Else.

"Is it wonderful? I think maybe I'm losing my mind!"

She had to go back at noon to handle the people in the dining room at Calvary House and I hated every brick in the place. "The devil take the people in the dining room at Calvary House!" I wanted to talk.

She was very loyal to Calvary House, though, and by the second day I was blackly jealous of all those who had to have Ellen on hand to tuck their napkins under their chins in the ever-present dining room. But I stayed on and we talked and talked and talked and talked and talked. She gave me *The Greatest Thing in the World* to read and it made me jealous of Henry Drummond and Ellen.

And then we talked through another day until it was Wednesday. I had not left my room once. I loved hotel rooms anyway and had lived in one alone and happy as a lark during the war when I worked out of New York for a while. But that was the Gladstone on Fifty-second Street near Fifth Avenue. This was sedate Gramercy Park and a very different New York.

I stayed in my room because I felt safer there. And anyway a big, puffing steam shovel made grinding noises and scattered dust outside and just down the block and across one street was "Calvary House"!

And Calvary Church.

And those people who had made Christ real to Ellen.

I was terribly nervous and smoked incessantly. And walked up and down my room *and,* when Ellen was on duty at mealtimes and after she went back to her room at night (promptly at eleven), I read the hotel Bible! I didn't plan to admit that to her at all.

At first I just lifted the front cover as it lay on the dresser there in its cheap, unattractive, black binding with the ugly insignia and thick red-edged pages. At first I just lifted the cover, flipped through a few pages, and put it in the drawer out of sight.

On Wednesday Ellen suggested casually (remembering how I had stormed at the idea that the Bible was anything more than just a great book) that I might be interested in reading the Gospels sometime. Something seemed always to stop her from pushing me—just in time.

After she left Wednesday night at eleven, I picked up the Bible and sat there holding it. She had said several times that my way of handling words and giving them new meanings in my poems reminded her of the style of writing in Ezekiel. I thought I'd look in the index and see if Ezekiel could be a book in the Bible. I had taken a course in the Bible as English literature in college and remembered that some of the books in the Bible were named after prophets. Ezekiel sounded as though he might easily have been a prophet. Lo, there he was in the index and when I turned to the Book of Ezekiel I was absolutely *charmed* by what I read! Somehow I landed in chapter forty right in the midst of the truly poetic description of the man "whose appearance was like the appearance of brass, with a line of flax in his hand and a measuring reed; and he stood at the gate."

I had no idea why he stood there or why he had to measure, but the lilt and music and simplicity of style of the chapter falling line on line into my delighted and suddenly relieved mind seemed to slip loose one knot after another within me. I read on through all his "measurings" of the "little chambers of one and six cubits" and exclaimed aloud when I came to this: "there were narrow windows to the little chambers, and to their posts within the gate round about, and likewise to the arches; and windows were round about inward: and upon each post were palm trees."

Could there be delightful things like this in THE BIBLE?

Chapter forty-one with the description of the temple intrigued me even more. I felt at home. Here was someone else who felt about words the way I did. Who was not content with giving them just one regular meaning. And he was an Old Testament prophet, of all people.

"Listen!" I said aloud, as I stood up and emoted alone there in the hotel room. "Listen to this!"

"And the side chambers were three, one over another, and thirty in order; and they entered into the wall which was of the house for the side chambers round about, that they might have hold. . . ."

(That was more extreme than anything I had ever written.)

"That they might have hold, but they had not hold in the wall of the house. . . ."

And then Ezekiel sang on with the music that charges with pure joy the soul of a writer wanting wings as I wanted them.

"And there was an enlarging, and a winding about still upward to the side chambers: for the winding about of the house went still upward round about the house: there the breadth of the house was still upward, and so increased from the lowest chamber to the highest by the midst. . . ."

I sat down and wept. Wagner and Beethoven used to hurt me

blissfully with too much music piled onto too much music, but it had been so long since I had allowed myself to be blissfully hurt like this. And here was an ancient prophet named Ezekiel hurting me again with a beauty that I had forgotten how to contain.

Ezekiel in the Bible!

Genie Price has gone stark, raving mad!

But I knew, oh, I knew that there *was* an enlarging, and a winding still upward . . . for the winding went *still upward*" . . . and I was caught in it! I feared it but I was glad to be caught in it. For the first time I almost understood what Ellen meant in the letter when she wrote, "This new thing isn't something you have. It is Something that *has* you."

*

The next morning I grabbed Ellen the minute she came in the door of my hotel room, sat her down, and hotel Bible in hand began to spout Ezekiel at her in excited tones.

I know now that what she really wanted to do was fall on her knees and say, "Thank You Lord. Oh, thank You! At last *You've* got her reading Your Word!"

But what she did, as far as I could see anyway, was to pick it all up apparently on my low level of mere excitement about the literary style and gently and without my suspecting a thing led me out of Ezekiel into first of all—Proverbs 8:22-36. I was so excited about Ezekiel I wanted to go on reading about his little chambers and cherubims and wheels but she had a way of getting my attention which she did not know at all until I told her in this book: always before she began to explain anything to me or to answer my usually difficult questions or as before she began to read from Proverbs, she—fell silent. Just for a few seconds, but it always made me feel as though she were—listening. And I wanted and always paid attention. She "listened" a moment and then began to read:

"The Lord possessed me in the beginning of his way, before his works of old. I was set up from everlasting, from the beginning, or ever the earth was. When there were no depths, I was brought forth; when there were no fountains abounding with water. Before the mountains were settled, before the hills was I brought forth: while as yet he had not made the earth, nor the fields, nor the highest part of the dust of the world. When he prepared the heavens . . .''

"Stop. Please stop. Just a minute." My heart felt squeezed.

"All right. Is anything wrong, Genie?"

"No. I— No, just makes me nervous to hear anyone else read."

"Then you finish it."

I took the Book from her and although my hands had never been one bit shaky on any morning after, I noticed particularly that they shook when I reached for the Bible.

"I was reading right there in verse twenty-seven. The beginning of verse twenty-seven . . . in the part about the heavens."

I lighted a cigarette and hoped Ellen hadn't noticed that I left one burning in the ashtray on the dresser. She did notice, of course, and in her quiet manner as though it were the least she could do for me, she walked over to the dresser and put it out.

"Verse twenty-seven, did you say?"

"Yes. That's where I stopped reading."

I always liked the way I read aloud, but my voice sounded as though it came back from a radio echo chamber as I began verse twenty-seven:

"When he prepared the heavens, I was there: when he set a compass upon the face of the depth: when he established the clouds above: when he strengthened the fountains of the deep: when he gave to the sea his decree, that the waters should not pass his commandment: when he appointed the foundations of the earth: Then I was by him, as one brought up with him: and I was daily his delight, rejoicing always before him; rejoicing in the habitable part of his earth; and my delights were with the sons of men."

I stopped reading. I was so short of breath. Then I looked at her and it was a moment with so much clinging to it!

"Ellen?"

"Yes?"

"Who is the 'I' in what we've been reading? No, first tell me— is the 'him' God?"

"Yes, the 'him' is God, the Father."

"Well, then who's the 'I'? Who was there when He set a compass upon the face of the depth?" I tried not to shout. "Who was there before the mountains were settled? Who's the 'I'?"

"Do you have any idea who it could be, Genie?"

"I suppose you're going to say it was Jesus Christ."

"Yes, it was."

"But in the first part of the chapter it says Wisdom is talking. I caught you that time. You're imagining things. You're on a Jesus Christ kick!"

"In the Scofield Reference Bible in a footnote on that part of Proverbs it says the Wisdom referred to is Christ."

"That's just somebody's interpretation. Mother used to have a Scofield Bible. How do you know Scofield is right?"

"He gives as his authority his own devout heart."

"His own devout heart?"

"Yes. He says quite simply that the devout mind is sure that this is Christ who was there in the beginning. There are certain things a Christian just knows. Like the Gospel of John—in the very first verse it says, "In the beginning was the word and the word was with God and the word was God. By him were all things made and without him was not anything made that was made."

"Is *that* in the Bible, too?"

"Yes, in the Gospel of John."

"Brother, those old birds could really write! That's magnificent!"

"Want to read the rest of Proverbs eight?"

"No, I want luncheon. Order for you, too?"

She smiled. "No thanks. You come eat with me today in the dining room."

"Are you kidding? It would take more than a few verses of Scripture to get me to eat with a bunch of Christians, dear heart. They scare me."

I tried the casual treatment, but somehow I knew I wasn't fooling her one bit. Things couldn't have been flailing inside me as they were without making marks on my face. And when she had gone, I forgot about ordering my own luncheon and began reading the hotel Bible again.

She had quoted that gorgeous bit from the Gospel of John. I looked in the index under "gospel" and didn't find it. So I started browsing in the vicinity of the Psalms. Psalm 23 looked warm and familiar when I passed it. I experimented and discovered I still remembered it. I spoke aloud alone.

"Wonder if I learned any more of this when I was a kid?" "For God so loved the world that he gave his only begotten Son, that whosoever believeth on him should not perish but have everlasting life." That was John 3:16! No doubt the same as the Gospel of John!

I felt very, very proud and pleased and thought I'd quote it for Ellen when she came back. Something fresh and clean and new had crept in. Something not unlike the dream about the garden and the children who laughed. I dropped the Bible on the floor by the big chair in front of the window and sat watching the steam shovel at work.

"For God so loved the world that He gave his only begotten Son, that whosoever believeth on him should not perish but have everlasting life."

There was more to it than this life. That I knew. The "more" almost had to be God, didn't it? But what could God be like? If only we had a picture of Him!

"God is everywhere" they had taught us in Sunday School. But that was one of the things that made me angry. Everywhere was far too vague.

Ellen came back that afternoon and stayed only about an hour because she had to do some book work for the eternal dining room. I had been trying to reach a friend of ours from Charleston who was in New York radio and before she left I reached him and invited him to bring a friend and come up for a drink.

This, of course, was to hurt Ellen. The drink part, I mean. She loved the boy from home as much as I did. She was very close to his mother.

She left and my guests came and I ordered drinks for them but could not order for myself. Naturally I had to explain. And what I said was, "I am either stumbling onto Reality or I'm on my way to a padded cell. It has to be one or the other."

The friend from home remarked effusively about how well I looked and didn't seem to doubt that something was happening. He seemed glad to leave in a little while.

When Ellen came back late in the afternoon, I really surprised her because I was dressed and wanted to take a walk in Gramercy Park. I had never wanted to take a walk in a park in my life before and I knew for sure then that much more than I meant to happen was happening.

But since it was my first park, it "did something for me" that she had access to the key to the big iron gate to Gramercy Park. It seems it is a very exclusive park and not really public at all unless you are a part of the "public" with a key.

It was certainly unlike the New York I had known, but what was difficult for me was that for moments some of the time *this* New York seemed more familiar than the other one which I had known before.

The friend who had visited me that afternoon said he was glad to see me looking so well and seeming to be so interested in life but he hoped I wouldn't go too far with this God thing. I told Ellen this in the park and she smiled.

Ellen and his mother had been praying for us both.

That night we had dinner in my room. I did not ask how the (to me) "nebulous" Christians in the dining room at Calvary House got along without her, but she says she will always remember that dinner we had together because I asked her to "ask the blessing" for the first time. I will always remember it, too, because she "listened" for the merest moment before she began and I knew she had caught His ear. I will always remember it, too, because it wasn't one of those memorized things people grind out and anyway I hadn't even heard one of those in fifteen years.

When Ellen gave thanks she talked right to God and called Him "You" and seemed to know Him personally and said things to Him about the two of us sitting there ready to eat.

That night before Ellen left to go to her room in Calvary House, she said:

"By the way, we didn't finish that gorgeous part of Proverbs yesterday."

"The part about things before the mountains were settled?"

"Why don't you finish that chapter after I go tonight?"

"What chapter was it?"

"Eight . . . verse twenty-two to the end of the chapter."

"You're being so patient with me. I'm very grateful."

"I'm grateful, too, Genie."

"Stay and talk to me some more about—Him."

"You believe He exists now, don't you?"

"Most of the time I do, yes. Please stay longer."

"He does exist *all* of the time, and it will be much better for you to let Him talk to you without me. And for you to talk to Him."

I laughed. "Me talk to God? Why, that's praying!"

"Yes, I know it is. Good night, Genie. I'll be back in the morning as soon as I can get here."

*

For the first time in my life I felt glad to do as I was told. And quite obediently I opened the Bible to Proverbs 8 and read silently the first verses we had read: twenty-two through thirty-one. Then I read thirty and thirty-one again aloud:

"Then I was by him, as one brought up with him: and I was daily his delight, rejoicing always before him; rejoicing in the habitable part of his earth; and my delights were with the sons of men."

". . . my delights were with the sons of men."

If the "I" in that passage did happen to be Christ speaking, as the Old Testament Wisdom, did that mean that He loved old New York and Chicago and other "habitable" places of the earth and that "His delights" were really with the sons of men?

That would mean me, if it were true!

Why did Ellen want me to *finish* that chapter particularly?

When I finished it I found out:

"Now therefore hearken unto me, O ye children; for blessed are they that keep my ways. Hear instruction, and be wise, and *refuse it not.* Blessed is the man that heareth me, watching daily at my gates, waiting at the posts of my doors. For whoso findeth me findeth life, and shall obtain favour of the Lord. But he that sinneth against me wrongeth his own soul: *all they that hate me love death.*''

After that I sat there for a long time and knew why she had asked me to finish the chapter.

''. . . he that sinneth against me wrongeth his own soul . . . but whoso findeth me findeth life. . . .''

Sometime after midnight, I reached for the Bible again. It wasn't nearly so ugly as it had been. I opened it to a book called Isaiah, chapter fifty-nine. But before I read any of that I happened to see the last verse of fifty-eight.

''Then shalt thou delight thyself in the Lord; and I will cause thee to ride upon the high places of the earth. . . .''

I? Would He cause *me* to ride upon the high places of the earth? Why? How? The beginning of the fifty-ninth chapter was next.

''Behold, the Lord's hand is not shortened, that it cannot save; neither his ear heavy, that it cannot hear.''

I hated the word ''saved.'' All the people I had ever known who went in for evangelism were always talking about saving souls. Intense, dreary people like those who stood on street corners and passed out those ugly tracts. People with inexcusable bad taste talked about being ''saved.'' Why did Isaiah have to spoil everything? The other parts of the Bible had been pure art!

But I rather liked the last part of the verse about ''neither is his ear heavy, that it cannot hear.'' That helped. Yes, I was pathetically touchy. But that's why I was there in the hands of the living God.

I *needed* so to be there! I needed so to be—saved.

Isaiah kept handing me strong, magnetic things and I took them eagerly and forgot ''saved.'' ''Their feet run to evil . . .''—yes, mine did. So what? ''The way of peace they know not; and there is no judgment in their goings.'' Mother used to say I showed poor judgment in things. ''. . . they have made them crooked paths: whosoever goeth therein shall not know peace . . . *we wait for light,* but behold obscurity; for brightness, *but we walk in darkness.*''

I had to stand up. I couldn't stop reading but I couldn't bear to sit down a minute longer. And I began again to read aloud alone.

"We grope for the wall like the blind, and we grope as if we had no eyes: we stumble at noon day as in the night; we are in desolate places as dead men. . . ."

No!

Then I was on my knees by the side of the bed sobbing:

"I am in a desolate place as a dead man!"

*

When I looked at my watch it was just 1:00 A.M. I had friends uptown in New York City who not only would have been hurt to know I was there and hadn't called them, but who would come and get me right now and take me back uptown where I belonged. Back to Fifty-second Street where the "rich people" with silver horns in their beautiful dark fingers made the world seem not out there to trouble you anymore.

Would I call someone or just dress and grab a cab and go? Perhaps to Nina's on Madison just off Seventieth? Maybe a producer I knew. Anywhere I could feel at home and relaxed and get away from this Thing that—followed me.

This Thing that hounded me.

The Hound of Heaven.

I dressed. And then limply I dropped my brown velvet hat with the veil on the bed and went back to the chair beside the window. I opened the Bible to the Psalms again. One hundred and nineteen was a long one. And as far as I know it was the Hebrew characters that headed each section which attracted my attention. But my voice sounded as though I had been sick for a long time when I began to read here and there in long Psalm 119 . . . aloud, alone.

"Blessed are they that seek him with the whole heart . . . O that my ways were directed to keep thy statutes!"

I hadn't noticed many exclamation points in the Bible, but there was one and well it should be where I was concerned. With *my* ways I could never keep His statutes! They were too hard. I could never, never live the way Ellen lived.

Never!

"Blessed are thou, O Lord, teach me thy statutes! Open thou mine eyes, that I may behold wondrous things out of thy law. *I am a stranger in the earth:* hide not thy commandments from me! . . . My soul breaketh . . . my soul cleaveth unto the dust: quicken thou me according to thy word. I have declared my ways, and thou heardest me: teach me thy statutes. Make me to understand the way of thy precepts: so shall I talk of thy wondrous works. My soul melteth for *heaviness:* strengthen thou me according to thy word. Remove from me the way of lying. . . ." There was not an exclamation point there but there should have been for me. ". . . remove from me the way of lying and grant me thy law graciously!"

I was on my knees again with the Bible open on the bed before me. I didn't know how to pray, but maybe God would listen if I just read to Him out of the Bible with all my heart.

"Thy hands have made me and fashioned me: give me understanding that I may learn thy commandments. Let my heart be sound in thy statutes; that I may not be ashamed. Make thy face to shine upon thy servant; and teach me thy statutes. Rivers of waters run down mine eyes, because they keep not thy law."

Rivers of waters ran down my eyes and wrinkled the pages of the hotel Bible and then I pushed it aside and tried to pray but all I could say was:

"O God . . . O God . . . O God . . . *O God!*"

*

About 5:00 A.M. I got up from my knees and lighted my first cigarette in almost four hours. I picked up the Bible again and read the very last verse of Psalm 119. Aloud.

"I have gone astray like a lost sheep; seek thy servant; for I do not forget thy commandments."

When I was barely four years old I stood in the pulpit of our church back home and sang *all* verses of the Ninety and Nine. Now and then through the years when I had enough to drink to tip the inside of my heart so the truth showed, I would sing the Ninety and Nine. At five in the morning there in the Gramercy Park Hotel before the steam shovel began to work that day, I sang what I could remember of the first verse:

> There were ninety and nine that da-da-da,
> In the shelter of the fold,
> But one was out on the hills away,
> Far off from da-da-da-da;

I remembered all of the chorus and also how hard it was for me to reach those high notes when I was four. Mother had said, "Don't strain, dear."

There was nothing *but* strain that morning . . . not of my voice, but of my soul.

> Away on the mountains wild and bare,
> Away from the tender Shepherd's care,
> Away from the tender Shepherd's care.

The strain of knowing suddenly that one is separated from God is the worst strain of all. Especially after one has lived so many years believing there is no God. To *realize Him and the space between* you at one and the same time is almost too much to bear.

It *is* too much to bear.

O God . . . O God . . . O God!

16

Another Telephone Call

"It *is* a fearful thing to fall into the hands of the living God." But all around the fear there brooded an almost familiar assurance that "my kindness shall not depart from thee." I hadn't read that promise in Isaiah yet, but although I knew I was going to crash, it seemed as though there would be kindness when it happened.

But the fear and the trembling and the strangeness and the heaviness must have shown black and deep on my face when Ellen arrived to spend Friday morning with me.

She looked tired, too, and I wanted to tell her how sorry I was to be causing her so much trouble but all I could say was:

"Something has happened to me."

"Do you know what it is?" She was very careful with me.

"No. But I'd give anything if I had never begun to believe in God! I'm coming apart at the seams."

The waiter brought my two big pots of black coffee and a fresh supply of cigarettes. I signed the check and he bowed out of the room and closed the door.

"Will this feeling ever go away now that I believe in Him?"

"Genie, *what* do you believe about God?"

I set the hotel coffee pot down too hard and snapped:

"How do I know *what* I believe? I just know He's—alive! That's enough to make me so miserable I'd gladly shoot myself."

I started to walk up and down the dark, maroon-patterned rug in front of the dresser.

"I can't 'keep his everlasting precepts'—I'm not put together that way!"

Ellen smiled at me. "Where did you read about precepts?"

"Last night. Statutes too. All night that Bible's been haunting me. But what happens now?"

"God will win."

"You mean I can't?"

"You can refuse to surrender to Him, but that won't mean you'll win. Everything will be harder and harder now that you've come this close to Him."

"Little Molly Sunshine just came to call."

"I'm sorry. I hate to hurt you. Or frighten you."

"Forget it. And how can you be so quiet about things? You sit there acting as though ghastly things like this happen every day. Don't you give a—?"

She turned her face away quickly and I was so sorry.

"Forgive me, Ellen. I'm sorry. And I'm so—tired!"

"Why don't you let it all end right now, Genie? He's got your attention. He won't stop until He's got you, too. Is your life so happy and so good that you won't take a chance on God's having something better? Something more exciting? Something that will really fill that emptiness inside you? If you're tired, don't you want to—rest?"

I looked at her and laughed what didn't turn out to be a real laugh at all.

"If you knew how many times I've passed cemeteries and longed to change places with the lucky stiffs lying there with nothing to do but *rest*, you'd never ask such a crazy question."

"I knew that."

"Hm."

"You may think it's one *thing* or another that you hate to give up. It's really yourself."

"But my work—a radio producer can't make a living without beer commercials and violence! If God objects as you say He does to people making a living, then I'm terribly sorry, I just can't—"

"That isn't what God objects to."

"But suppose a beer sponsor wants a show and he comes to me?"

"That's a marginal issue. Lots of Christians disagree on lots of marginal issues."

"More alibis, huh?" I was accusing myself.

"More excuses for hanging on to the most important person in the world."

"Don't be nasty, dear. It isn't Christian."

"I'm not being nasty. Until I was off my own hands into the hands of the living God I *was* the most important person in the world to—Ellen Riley. And right now you're fighting God because Eugenia Price is the most important person in the world to you."

"I could never keep the Ten Commandments! I'm too old!"

"You're only thirty-three, but you couldn't keep them even if you were only twenty-three or thirteen. Neither could I."

"But you do. You're a saint."

"Righteousness is a pure *gift* of Grace."

"Don't start with that theological bosh. I don't understand it."

She "listened" a minute and then said very quietly:

"If you will just turn around and begin to follow Jesus Christ this minute, He'll see to it that you *can* keep the Ten Commandments and more. That's His part. That is (if you'll pardon the expression) Grace."

"I don't want to talk about Jesus Christ."

"He's God's revelation of Himself."

"I can't swallow that."

"You mean you don't want to."

"Who knows what I mean, you or I?" She didn't answer me. But she looked so concerned and I felt so ashamed. More than I had the other times when I snapped at her or used Jesus Christ's name to punctuate my railings at God and at life. I made frequent use of Christ's name. And that seemed to hurt Ellen more than anything I said to her. No matter how unkind. This annoyed me and I thought she was being sanctimonious. Practically everybody used His name when they swore. Didn't they?

Of course I knew she wasn't being sanctimonious because she always tried not to let me see that expression at all. We drank coffee for a few minutes in silence and then I said:

"Maybe if I called Mother and told her I had discovered God that would hold my nose to the fire and I'd just have to surrender to Him!"

She told me later that she wanted so much to be sure I realized first that the *only* Way to the Father was through the Son, Jesus Christ. But Something kept her silent. She just seemed to sit there and yearn for my peace of heart and mind. I wanted desperately for her to say something.

"Do you think that would make me do it if I called Mother?"

"I know how much she has influenced you always. She's been your god in a way. What do you think she would say?"

"Oh, Mother's religious. She's been saying I should go to church. She's watched me fall apart these last two years and all the poor woman dared to say was 'find a nice church and start going, dear.' "

"I know your mother wants only the best for you, Genie."

"What do you think? No, never mind what you think! I'm going to send her a telegram right now and tell her I'll be calling her tonight long distance with the most important telephone call of my life!"

"Well, what will you tell her when you call?"

I almost ran my coffee cup over. "I don't know what I'll tell her but maybe just the fact that after I send the wire I'll have to call and say *something* will force me to—*do it* between now and eleven o'clock tonight."

"Why eleven o'clock?"

"Oh, no reason. Mother and I just always have called each other at eleven o'clock. There are some telegraph blanks here in the desk. I'm going to send it fast and then it will be too late to back down."

Ellen looked at me with endless love as I scribbled the message on the yellow blank. "You really *want* to belong to Him, don't you, Genie?"

"Something's got to happen. I can't stand much more of this."

"You couldn't prove your intentions more than sending that wire to your mother."

I finished writing the message and reached for the telephone to get a bellboy. The old Genie Price was dying hard. *She* raised an eyebrow and remarked:

"Of course, I can always lie when I call her tonight. Very plausible that I'm in New York on 'business.' The 'important telephone call' could very nicely be a big new show. Mother and Dad wouldn't be surprised or even pay much attention by now. I've been making 'the most important telephone call of my life' to them for years. Poor darlings. I'm certainly glad I'm *their* daughter and not mine.''

The telegram saying that I would call them for the most important telephone call of my life went winging to Charleston. Collect, of course. And between that afternoon and eleven o'clock that night, only the Grace Ellen talked about kept me from flying into a million tiny pieces.

*

At exactly five minutes to eleven that evening Ellen walked out the door of my room. I was both relieved and dismayed that she did not wait to be sure I told Mother the truth. But she left and somehow the very fact that she did made me all the more certain that she was right when she said she was leaving me there with Him. I knew He would be listening.

I addressed myself as sixteen different varieties of fool for having gotten into this call-to-Mother business in the first place. And sitting on the bed by the telephone stand I lighted a cigarette in preparation for the ordeal, smoked about a third of it, put it out, and lighted another one, also in preparation for the ordeal.

Ordeal? Calling Mother hadn't been that before.

But this time was this time and very, very different from any other time in my whole life. The operator said that Genie Price was calling from New York collect and, as always, before the operator finished her speech, Mother said, ''Yes, indeed, we certainly will accept the charges.''

This split second while Mother greeted me in her special cheerful long-distance telephone voice I loved so much was my last chance to fabricate a ''reason'' for having called. I was adept at fabrication and a split second had been ample time for years, but instead I blurted:

''Mother, I think I've discovered what God is all about!''

During that long, God-watched moment when we both just breathed on our separate ends of the wire, it hit me that I *had* only gone *that*

far and no further. *I had not surrendered to God.* I had only fallen
into His hands and was still fighting Him with all my wits. Wanting
Him with my heart but fighting Him with my wits.

"Have you made a decision, dear?"

I hadn't heard Mother mention a "decision" since I was fourteen
and playing for the revival meetings at church. It sounded strange
and unlike Mother and very very much like Mother, too.

"A decision?" My laugh was nervous. "No. Not yet. But I thought
maybe if I called you I'd somehow have to do it! I want to, Mother.
I really want to live for God. Do you think I'm crazy? Will Dad and
Joe think I'm crazy?"

Mother had begun to cry. "Are you in New York City with Ellen,
dear? At the place where she lives?"

"No. I'm scared of that place. It's full of Christians, but I'm with
her. I mean I've been spending a lot of time with her. She's so
doggone peaceful, Mother. And I'm tired of trying to be something
I'm not!"

"How's your money, dear?" The most familiar question of all.

"Low as usual. I'm going home tomorrow. Back to Chicago."

"No. Daddy will wire you a hundred dollars. I want you to stay
there and be exposed to Ellen over the weekend. Daddy will want
you to stay, too."

The money came the next morning and I stayed over. On Saturday
afternoon further proof came that something *was* happening in me.

I went the last place I ever dreamed I'd go. To Calvary House to
see Ellen's room and write Mother a note on one of the office
typewriters. Ellen promised not to introduce me to anyone if she
could avoid it, and I went. It was like a big college dormitory, only
it had an elevator. I said it was gloomy and must be convenient for
people with very little money. That's what I said, but I felt a movement
and a Life there that was brand new to me.

And attractive.

I didn't feel one bit at home, but I wanted to.

We may have used the private key and walked again in the little
locked-up Gramercy Park but neither of us remembers whether we

did or not. I simply remember a kind of lull in things and a waiting and a restlessness that had tears in it. But I remember how sweet the air seemed and Ellen was even kinder than usual and very, very careful with me.

It was as though we both knew something tender and eternal was about to happen.

In fact, I began to wish I knew exactly what to do about it but Ellen just seemed to be "listening" and I felt somehow the way young girls must feel when they are about to be married.

I had not confessed that Jesus Christ is Lord, but the Holy One of Israel had my attention. My full attention. So much so that, even before Ellen asked me, I said I wanted to go to church with her the next morning, which was Sunday.

She said I would have to wear a hat, which I hated to do, but for some reason I had brought one with me and so I said I'd wear it. She was supposed to come to the hotel to get me at about ten o'clock so we would have time to talk a little and get there early. She wanted me to be there before the eleven o'clock service started, she said, because there was one old window she wanted me to see. There were elegant new ones, too, but this old one was the one she wanted me to see.

It was beautiful and misty green and small and up in a high, vaulted corner, as I remember it. A big square Cross was tipped sideways in its design of heavy clouds. Light came from the Cross in rays as it burst through the clouds. Rays that had the help of the Sunday morning sun outside.

I looked and looked and looked at that window.

And particularly at the Cross in it. And the heavy clouds.

This was the apparent reason she wanted us to be there early but also she knew *He* could get "at me" there in the silence of the old Calvary Church sanctuary. Could get "at me" off my own familiar territory.

I was very quiet and kept looking also at Ellen's hands while she sat in silent prayer. I knew they hadn't always looked so peaceful. But they did now. And my heart longed for that peace. My hands were restless without a cigarette.

This was the first church service I had attended in eighteen years. I went to my Grandmother Price's funeral but that was all. Dr. Shoemaker spoke simply and with beautiful diction and deep humility about the Grace of Jesus Christ.

There it was again. The *Grace of Jesus Christ!*

I couldn't tell Dr. Shoemaker to stop talking about Christ as I had told Ellen. And anyway I didn't want him to stop. He said Grace was a gift. That we only had to be empty to receive it. That Jesus had sacrificed Himself on the Cross of Calvary not only to atone for our sins once and for all, but to release Grace that was all-sufficient for anything. And that we only had to *receive* the Atonement *and* the Grace. At least this is what I remember of his sermon.

I wanted it to be true but whether I believed it or not I cannot say. All I can say is that when he had finished talking about Christ, Dr. Shoemaker, with a heavenly light on his face, prayed in his beautiful diction and when he talked to God in the name of Jesus Christ I longed to be able to do it, too. He was on very close terms with God. So was Ellen. They were at peace. Dr. Shoemaker obviously was an extremely intelligent, highly educated man. And yet he lived his life following the Carpenter of Nazareth. He said he was indwelt with God's Holy Spirit. He said anyone could be who belonged to Christ.

I don't know how much I believed but I know I longed to belong, too. And when it was time for Communion I thought:

"Ellen has been so kind and so patient with me, maybe if I go up there and kneel down and take Communion beside her it will help make up for all the trouble I've been. And also for that nasty crack I made about the grape juice when we first met in August."

Something was said about baptism, but I wasn't listening and I figured no one would know who I was anyway. So I got up and started to follow Ellen down the gently sloping center aisle toward the altar.

She avoided looking at me.

I felt as though I were going to faint and then I was jerked to a dead stop. No one had touched me. But I couldn't move a step nearer that altar where the Communion cup and the wafers waited to be shared by those who followed Christ.

"His Blood which was shed for thee."

"His Body which was broken for thee."

I turned and ran from the church and headed for the bar of the Gramercy Park Hotel! It was closed until 1:00 P.M. on Sunday! Ellen had to work at the church until 2:30 P.M. I had time with nothing to do. And so, while I waited for the bar to open, I walked round and round the block past Calvary Church and watched the people come out after the Communion service. A few noticed a nervous woman in a brown suit and a brown velvet hat standing across the street smoking one cigarette after another. A few noticed but New Yorkers and Chicagoans don't notice anyone for long.

So these were Christians. Did I want to be one? Ellen had said there were varying degrees of Christians. Many didn't go all the way with Christ. Many just came to church because it was the respectable thing to do. I thought that was revolting. If I were a Christian I'd want to be a—disciple.

"I'd want to kiss His feet with the nail prints in them!"

Did I say that?

Yes, I did. Aloud on the sidewalk across the street from the Church where the people were coming out to go home after Communion.

But I went back to my hotel and waited in the attractive lounge for the bar to open. About thirty-five minutes I waited. Hotels like this one were so much more attractive than gloomy places like churches.

"I belong here in this atmosphere. Not over there in that dingy place."

Then I remembered the little window with the Cross high in the vaulted corner of the old sanctuary and I thought about Grace. What a strange word for a minister to use. For the Bible to use for that matter. Grace to me had always meant to be graceful. I began turning the word *graceful* around in my mind as I waited.

"To be graceful meant to be filled with grace."

Dr. Shoemaker had said Grace was a gift. Released to us because Christ died for us on the Cross.

Christ.

Three minutes to one and I was waiting to walk in when the waiter who had given me room service opened the doors of the Gramercy Park cocktail lounge.

17

The Second Time

I sat there in the bar until almost two and then went to my room and ordered a large, expensive meal sent up. I asked the waiter to wait while I poured into a water glass the two double Scotch old-fashioneds I had ordered. I wanted him to take the old-fashioned glasses back with him so Ellen wouldn't see them when she came in after her own noon meal was over.

The water glass which contained the two drinks had been washed in very hot water and stood innocently empty on my room-service table when she knocked at my door a few minutes later. She looked apprehensive and was so sorry she couldn't get there sooner. I knew she would be wondering about me because she had seen me run from the church.

She was very, very, very careful with me. I recognized that careful treatment by then and because I had stopped off downstairs I was prone to express myself freely. And too glibly. And very like a phony. Which in part I still was.

"Your church service was very impressive, darling. Shoemaker could have gone far in the theater. The entire thing was good drama."

She just looked at me.

"In fact, I'm quite excited about this whole Christian business."

"Are you?" She sounded far away. On that opposite shore, the way she had sounded the first day we talked in August.

I beat the top of my cigarette with my forefinger.

"I'm not doing a very good job of this, am I?"

"No." I was suddenly afraid again for the first time since I "dropped in" downstairs. I knew she knew I had "dropped in," too. "No, you're not doing a very good job." She seemed quietly pleased that I wasn't.

68

"Ellen . . . ?"

"What is it?"

"What does God look like to you? What do you think of when you think of God?"

"I've told you. I think of Jesus Christ."

I began to walk up and down and it was very frustrating because my loaded room-service table was in the way. Suddenly I grabbed up the old cocky manner and raised my left eyebrow which I always did when I wanted to appear poised:

"Maybe you're right about Jesus Christ. Maybe He *is* God. Maybe they're one and the same."

"Genie!"

"Maybe that's true. And in church today I realized when I heard your minister speak that Christians don't need to be dull people as I thought. I think Jesus Christ is the most attractive Person I've ever known about. In fact, He's just what we've all been hunting for back in Chicago all these years. I and all my friends back there. We're all bored to death and He's tremendously exciting! *But*—I think *you're* far too radical about it. You say I'll have to give myself up entirely and I think that's emotionalism on your part. Or dramatics."

She stood up and was very tall for a moment.

"I didn't say that. Christ said it. It isn't my idea to give yourself up entirely. It's His."

"Well, then your interpretation is wrong. Extreme. Radical. Jesus Christ is just what we've all been hunting for back in Chicago, only it's ridiculous to say a man or a woman can't worship God and still be human. Certainly God can adapt Himself more easily than I can adapt myself!"

"Jesus Christ will *change* you, Genie, if you are willing. It's not a matter of adaptation! Have you missed the point completely?"

"No! On the contrary. And I can't wait to get back to tell my friends what I've discovered about God!"

Ellen walked toward me.

"Are you going back to Chicago and tell those people that twisted, distorted spiel about God adapting Himself to *your* way of life?"

I stepped back from her and stuck my chin out and laughed.

"I most certainly am. I think it's a fascinating idea! Christ should brighten things up for us considerably!"

She looked at me for a moment and then reached for her coat. It was a yellow tweed topper. Something pushed hard against my heart. I gripped my cigarette so tightly it broke and I had to put it out. Even that was gone for this walled-off moment before my last defense cracked. . . .

She wouldn't dare leave me now!

Ellen had her coat on and was at the door.

She had been so patient and long-suffering she couldn't go. But she was going and I knew that if she left me then I'd be without God forever.

God!

"Oh, God, don't let her go!" I didn't say this aloud. It screamed through my tightened heart. She hadn't turned the doorknob yet, and suddenly she walked back toward me across the room.

"It won't work any other way except His way, Genie. Jesus says He is the way and the truth and the life. He says no man cometh to the Father but by Him. Jesus Christ said that. And He's either telling the truth or He's the biggest phony who ever walked the face of the earth! He also says if we try to save our lives we'll lose them. But if we lose them for His sake we'll find them. We find life in Christ, Genie!"

". . . whoso findeth me findeth life!"

I remembered that from the end of the only part of Proverbs I know.

". . . whoso findeth *me* findeth life!"

The earth slipped a little beneath me as I stood there clutching the edge of the dresser until my finger with the bitten nail hurt. Ellen didn't smile at all.

"Genie, you'll make such a terrific Christian!"

I twisted around and fell into the big chair by the window and sobbed: "Oh, God, I wish I were dead!"

Ellen didn't come over and put her arm around me the way you would think at a time like that. Instead she said very calmly and with absolute authority:

"Genie, it would be wonderful if you *would* die!"

"What?"

"It would be the most wonderful thing that ever happened to you if the old Genie Price would die right now—this minute, so the new one can be born."

I stopped sobbing, I think.

We don't remember.

And after a few long seconds, Ellen says I looked up at her. The darkness dropped away and I whispered:

"Okay, I guess you're right."

Then light.

*

Ellen has wondered many times since then if what she did was right. Rather what she did not do. We didn't pray. I was so touchy and Ellen had never led anyone to Christ before. And anyway I had been praying out of Isaiah and the Psalms and wordless cryings of my own all week long. This was just the step into freedom and neither of us did anything after it. We just sat there that autumn afternoon in the peace and the quiet of His Presence and let Him be all around us. That I was truly born again from above no one has ever doubted.

The rest of the book is about a new child of God who had absolutely *everything* to learn. Everything, that is, except that Jesus Christ did come out of that tomb.

I knew that.

And I was so grateful that I knew it.

Ellen says she knew it in a new way at that moment, too. He couldn't still be in the tomb. He was there with us!

Part Two

———— ❖ ————

"UNSHACKLED!"

18

Train on Wings

I was born the first time on June 22, 1916, and then I was born the second time on October 2, 1949. And if this sounds like fantasy still to you, *this* is the part of the book which proves that the second birth is fact. And especially Reality.

*

On Monday morning, October 3, 1949, Ellen went to New York's Grand Central Station with me and put me on a train for Chicago and her faith in Christ leaped up. It had to. There would be no one to "feed the new babe" when she got there! A letter she wrote to me later that same morning said:

"I went back to my room at Calvary House and got on my knees to pray, but instead I just cried and cried and cried. And then He was bigger than He had ever been to me."

She cried in part from exhaustion, I'm sure. But she also knew what *could* happen to me without Christian "fellowship." (A word she knew better than to use, by the way, because my touchiness was far from gone.) She wept from weariness and concern and from the impact of that sudden up-leap of faith within her.

Ellen cried, but I sat up on the train in the coach all the way and scarcely knew it because to me the train had wings! As a first "birthday" gift, Ellen had handed me Thomas Kelly's *Testament of Devotion*, and she did it on direct orders from the Holy Spirit, because I don't think I put it down all the way back to Chicago except to look up at the stars now and then and say to God over and over, "You *are* real and now You're mine and now I'm Yours!" Thomas Kelly's writing and thinking had been influenced by Alfred North Whitehead and so had mine when I was in my early twenties and writing the

75

poetry. And with the single-simplicity and light in each line of *Testament of Devotion* I felt more and more at home. I didn't understand much of it yet, but I knew Thomas Kelly was my brother in Christ and, even though he had died physically a few years before, one day further along in this "Eternal Now" we could sit down and have good talk together. I had only believed in eternal life for a very few days, and I relaxed to know that Thomas Kelly who felt exactly as I did about both Christ *and* words would be there when I got there. Thomas Kelly and Ellen and Dr. Shoemaker did much to "redeem" Christians for me.

As the crack streamliner moved through the night toward Chicago, my heart leaped up with joy. The joy He promised His disciples. Was I a disciple of Jesus Christ? Yes! O Holy One of Israel . . . O Wonderful, O Wonderful, O Wonderful . . . Thou art only and art all! Thou art mine and I am Thine!

Thomas Kelly wrote of Holy Obedience. My soul called back: "Yes, I, too, want to be wholly obedient!"

I wanted to obey someone for the very first time in my entire life.

I had no idea what Holy Obedience would mean, but at that point the Holy One kept me mercifully blind to that. He knew I could not bear to see yet. He simply *filled* my soul with hunger to *belong to Him*. A hunger so deep and so wide that only He could fill it . . . I would follow Him anywhere. Anywhere. If only He is up ahead, I will follow.

"Where He leads me, I will follow . . . where He leads me, I will follow . . . Where He leads me, I will follow . . . I'll go with Him, with Him . . . all the way!"

For the first time in eighteen years I remembered that old song, and I longed to be able to run and tell someone I remembered it. There on the train I began to experience the pangs of longing for the companionship of other Christians who were also excited about Jesus Christ.

My eyes filled with quick tears for just a moment when it struck me for the first time that Ellen would be living in New York and I'd be in Chicago! Why had I waited all week long to become a

Christian when we could have been talking about Jesus instead of me?

People in Chicago would think I'd taken leave of my sanity. And they would have every reason to think that.

"I wonder what my friends *will* say?"

While I made the changeover from the old life to the new, I had arranged to spend a few days in the home of three friends who were devout Catholics. Surely they would understand what had happened to me. They believed in God. I wondered what they believed *about* Him? I didn't know much of what I believed, but I knew I was excited about Him and that we belonged to each other. I knew so many people, but it had been years since I had discussed God from a religious standpoint with anyone. I knew these friends at whose home I would stay went to Mass every Sunday morning. They would be excited when I burst in their front door and announced, "I have just discovered God! I'm a new creature in Christ Jesus. It says so in the Bible! I'm all new and never going to be the old Gene Price again!"

Yes, it was good to be going to their house for several days. I had so much studying and thinking and planning to do. And so much reading! I didn't own a Bible but I knew they would have one. I could scarcely wait to get there to begin reading it.

In the old days I probably would have helped myself to the hotel Bible as one did hotel towels and laundry bags. But that was out of the question now. I was a Christian! After all, hadn't I stood five minutes before I checked out waiting for the hotel cashier to find the slip I'd signed for four packages of Camels? I was a Christian! I couldn't cheat the Gramercy Park Hotel tobacco counter out of money. As I rode along the train, I remembered what I said to Ellen that morning as we stood waiting for the cigarette check at the cashier's window.

"You see, my new religion is costing me money already!"

I went back to Thomas Kelly and the train went on to Chicago.

19

"Go Quickly and Tell!"

Two things I had promised Ellen before I left New York. Number one: I would never begin a single day without at least half an hour of "quiet time" each morning with Him.

"Read something in the Bible first to cleanse and fill your mind and then just sit with Him in the silence."

This sounded like little enough to do, and the first time I managed to "sit with Him in the silence" for four entire minutes.

But I have kept that promise faithfully and now an hour and a half in God's Word, in prayer and listening is swift.

Promise number two: "Tell people what has happened to you."

I began keeping the second promise the minute I burst in the front door of my friends' house early the morning of October 4, 1949. They were receptive and wondering and very kind to me. One said she thought I must have received some special Holy "revelation."

They let me read their mother's well-worn old Douay Version of the Bible and I did little else for three or four days except to write long, excited, "spiritual" letters to Ellen. I was discovering things Eternal so fast I ate only to be polite and for the first time in fifteen years looked forward to waking up in the mornings. This I did at a frightfully early (to me) eight o'clock without an alarm!

I read and read and read the four Gospels. John at once became my favorite and still is. Perhaps because more than anything I, too, wanted to be Jesus' "beloved disciple." His love held me completely captive.

Little I knew in my own life of the meaning of "cruciform and blood-stained" but the thought of my Beloved hanging on a Cross made me weep and want to hang there with Him.

I went to church with my friends once and the Stations of the Cross hurt me and held me and I wept because He had to die for me. And yet I knew *life* had *found me*! Glorious, sun-filled, Son-blinded life that would never let me go. This was not masochistic torment into which I walked with chin held high, determined to serve my Beloved, even if I had to stifle my own desires and shut out the call of a dark-melodied world. This was not a walk of self-effacement and ecstatic torment. This was a command to return to childhood!

This was a call back to the Natural.

This was my Creator calling me into the joy of Oneness with Him! This was "from the beginning, or ever the earth was" and this was new.

This was a completely *new* life. Just created *in* me. I had not learned to walk in it yet. But it was mine as eternity was mine. And for the first time in many years, those short crisp lines as in my early poetry began to move to the surface of my mind.

Joyfully!

> I search
> The secret
> Silence
> Of my soul
> For some
> New way
> To say:
> I love.
>
> An outward
> Turn back
> To the old
> Is not
> Nor will
> It ever be,
> For now
> Is *Now*.
>
> So spring
> I inward
> Where the
> Light is

Ever held at
Springing
And Eternity
And Love
And All
Are mine
At last.

For the first three days after I came back to Chicago I just read the Bible, prayed, walked in the falling autumn leaves and wrote and wrote and wrote.

There I was back on the South Side of Chicago again, not far from where I had found "Near Reality" ten years before on Cornell Avenue. My friends lived not many blocks from my old apartment. The South Side smelled the same in autumn because there are trees out there and people actually burn leaves in the gutters the way people who write sonnets love for them to do. I loved the burning leaves, too, and I loved not minding admitting to something I considered suitable material only for poets who rhymed things.

Slowly the high walls of having to be one certain way or *smother* began to vanish. I had smothered and was free. I found myself talking with people on the streets again. I hadn't dreamed of ever getting into another sidewalk discussion now that Spunky was gone. I didn't like them then but I couldn't resist because people admired her so much and I was so proud of her. But there I was ambling along the sunny, leaf-smoked Hyde Park streets smiling at people and talking to them at the slightest opportunity.

Did I really love them?

Yes, I did.

Oh, yes, I really did!

October 7, 1949

Ellen, dear . . .

You know it's the most amazing thing the way I love people now! I don't have to work on it either. It's just in my heart.

October 8, 1949

Dear Genie,

I was wondering last night if you have told any of your other old friends about your conversion to Christ. If so, what did they say?

After the first three days I began to *tell* it. It wasn't that I meant to wait even that long. I just needed that time to grasp some of it myself. And then I began the rounds of my old friends and the heads of the various radio networks and advertising agencies where I had professional contacts.

They all listened attentively with reactions which ranged from misty eyes to raised eyebrows—Jews, Catholics, pagans, occasional churchgoers, skeptics, agnostics. My "audience" varied more each day it seemed and the more I told about it, the more I knew it was true.

Witnessing for Jesus Christ is supposed to be very difficult, but I didn't know that, and so I found it all extremely stimulating and exciting and not one bit difficult as it is supposed to be. I knew none of the stock phrases then, and so must have startled everyone considerably as I breezed in and out one agency waiting room after another network lobby, beaming and declaring:

"I've fallen in love with God!"

"You what?"

"I have a new Romance! This one begins with a capital R."

"Yeah?"

"Yes! I'm in love with Jesus Christ. And look, I want you to watch me from now on. I don't understand it either, but according to the Bible I'm a new creature and I won't be doing the things I used to do because I belong to Christ now and He belongs to me!"

"Don't worry, old girl. You'll be watched. Like a hawk."

I was. And nothing is more conducive to spiritual growth than the knowledge that skeptical people who don't know Him are watching your every move.

Early, very early, I was made aware that everywhere I went I had the reputation of Jesus Christ in my hands.

And within two weeks I had turned down a high-salaried TV dramatic show and closed Eugenia Price Productions, because I could not write murder stories for children to watch nor talk adults into doing what I could no longer do and follow my new Lord. Not and belong to Him as I had to belong. Came and departed the week of swift tie-breaking. And by October twentieth I was free of every professional tie except a large indebtedness to an elderly lady who had graciously loaned me money when I first opened the office.

Did I say free? Yes, free and broke and far, far in debt. But I was beginning to remember what I read in my Bible, and Ellen reminded me in at least every other letter that if I would seek Him and His Kingdom first "all these things" would be added unto me.

Did I take that literally?

Completely.

And for another week all I seemed able to do was sit out on the black and white sun porch of my kind friends' home and read the Word of God.

What would I do next? I had no idea.

How would I earn a living? I had no ideas whatever.

Could I continue in radio and still be a Christian? I didn't know and that week I seemed unable to concentrate on it. I had so much to learn about Him. He was my Saviour and my Lord and my Beloved and I knew so little about Him. Over and over and over I read things He had said.

"If any man would be my disciple, let him deny himself, take up his cross daily and follow me."

Only God would dare say that! What a relief that He *is* God.

"Come unto me all ye that labour and are heavy laden and I will give you rest."

Only God *could give* rest.

"Take my yoke upon you, and learn of me; for I am meek and lowly in heart: and ye shall find rest unto your souls. For my yoke is easy and my burden is light."

". . . *my yoke is easy, and my burden is light*"!

Early I was able to believe that because He said it.

If He said it, it just had to be true because of who He is.

Jesus said His yoke is easy and His burden is light. So, even though for the first time I *wanted* a clean slate financially, I knew

I must not fret and stew if I had no job and no idea of how I would pay my debts. I knew I must wait on God, then obey Him.

As I look back over almost five years, this takes my breath away. Figuring angles had been my life. And yet there I sat reading the Gospel of Matthew as carefree as a child in her father's house.

The *one* thing I did for which I can take credit was to *believe* that I had become a child in my Father's house. I believed it and I saw no reason not to *act* like it.

A carton of cigarettes began to last a very long time. My daily average dropped from a frequent three packs to less than one. It hadn't occurred to me at all that He might want me to stop smoking. Practically everyone I knew smoked except Mother, who didn't like the taste of tobacco, and two of the friends with whom I was staying. But one night while I was still their guest, I lay in bed praying and at the same time smoking a last cigarette for the night. Prayer was so new to me I had formed a habit of picturing a railroad track from Heaven to Earth and on that "track" which was my faith, He was able to send down the answer. Suddenly the "track" seemed all smoke-filled and hazy and cut off. And aloud I said, "Lord, could it be that You don't want me to smoke?"

To me cigarettes were like my breath and next to it in importance. I loved them. I began smoking when I was fourteen and almost twenty years had passed since then. They were a great emotional satisfaction as they are to everyone who smokes habitually. I do not say the use of tobacco will make "void" your passage to Heaven. I am simply telling you what happened to me.

I had to stop. And I did, the first of several times, that night— with that cigarette which I was smoking as I prayed. I put it out and said, "All right, Lord," and He drew closer.

Then I got right out of bed and went into the kitchen and told my friends what I had done. They wondered and admired me and for the first time in my life I didn't want to be admired at all. My only part had been to obey. But I did learn that our part is to be *willing* to go right through suffering *with* Him. There is a great Glory in the fellowship of His sufferings. It brings Oneness with Him. And the more Oneness, the more Glory and the more Glory, the more Oneness.

But His heart longs for us to have fellowship with His *Resurrection Life!* And it is well for us to learn, more completely than I learned then, that even He did not have to hang on the Cross after He died.

Every time I gave up something for Him, I loved Him more. And as He walked with me through those stumbling, blundering first days in which He was testing my sincerity, He *kept* me aware of His actual presence. I believe He did this because He knew how unaccustomed I was to considering God at all.

Certainly He, most of all, knew how tricky I had always been. He could not move forward with His Plan for my life until He had given me a few preliminary trials. And even though He knew I had not yet given up the "right" to myself, He did know that I had confessed Him as my Lord and Saviour . . . that I had stopped smoking and, of course, I had stopped drinking . . . that I had stopped believing worry necessary to daily life . . . that I longed to be with other people who loved Him as I did . . . that my chief happiness was reading things He said . . . that I didn't understand it at all, but that I knew I had been *made new.*

He knew I was waiting for Him now.

And He moved.

A letter came from Ellen written in a high excitement. But so definite and certain. One thing had happened and then right after it another thing had changed in her work and when a third thing happened right after the second, she knew what to do. In this letter I learned for the first time how strong her compelling to come to Chicago to "look after me" had been. And now she was at peace about it. Providential circumstances had cut her ties in New York and she was coming to Chicago to be with me!

It was October, but I sang "Joy to the World!" I didn't know many Christian songs at that point, but I knew "Joy to the World." And I sang it as loudly as I could sing it and kissed all three of my hostesses and kissed my pocket-picture of Jesus over and over and over and over.

Now I'd be able to find out all the wonderful things Ellen knew about Him! I'd rush right out and rent an apartment and we'd read the Bible and talk about Jesus Christ twenty-four hours a day the rest of our earthly lives!

I still lived under the sign of an exclamation point and overdid everything, but every exaggerated intention was toward Him and, as you will see, He blessed and transformed and *used* my every blunder.

He knew he had reached down and saved an immature, "spoiled-brat" extremist. But He knew He had saved her and now He would begin to make her like Himself.

We didn't know it, but He knew all along that the first thing He had to do, of course, was to send Ellen to Chicago so He could continue the process through her, which He had so breathtakingly begun.

20

Blunder to Transform

There is one mansion-lined, shady street on the Near North Side of Chicago which is considered by everyone to be the most elegant street on the entire North Side. Particularly is it considered to be the most elegant by those who live up and down it in mahogany-paneled "brownstones," balconied "smooth stones," large glass front "moderns" and old ivy-covered "red bricks."

In answer to an ad which read "English basement, —— Street, nothing comparable," I went to look with a friend who had many misgivings, but knew how hard apartments were to find in Chicago in 1949. The building was one of the loveliest brownstones. Light brownstones, in fact, newly sandblasted. And inside in the owner's apartment, my heart sang, "Thank You Lord!" It was beautiful. But my friend had *seen* the one for rent which was "comparable to nothing," according to the ad in the paper. And as the owner (an altogether amazing blond lady in riding breeches) gestured sweepingly for us to follow her "downstairs," I saw at once that only the upstairs had been given the remodeling touch that makes a run-down mansion an elegant home.

Downstairs there *was* "nothing comparable."

The blond, jodhpured owner was doing an admirable job of keeping my mind occupied with herself. But in spite of her high ability, I did see the "apartment." I should be ashamed to admit that I saw it because I signed a year's lease to rent it at one hundred and twenty-five dollars per month. But I do admit I saw it and immediately leaped wildly and innocently to a completely *wrong* spiritual conclusion.

"This," I breathed to myself (remembering Thomas Kelly's thought about the Inward Light in which everything appears in an entirely new relationship), "is no doubt God's idea for me! I've been so high and mighty all my life, most likely He wants me to learn to live in peasant surroundings like this!''

I feel positive God never wills for any of His children to go head over heels in debt for something which is sheer madness in the first place. But following my wrong "guidance" all the way, with childlike abandon of the few practical maturities I had inadvertently gathered through the years, I made a profound statement about the Lord taking care of His own, misquoted the Scripture about Seek ye first the Kingdom and signed the lease with a flourish almost "comparable" to the owner's own.

With that flourish I sentenced Ellen and myself to one year in a literal dungeon. There was one pipe-paneled, pipe-ceilinged room about ten by fifteen feet, of dark, pocketbook brown with green and yellow candelabra (*with* flames) *painted* on one wall and a purple rooster on the other. Also around the crooked doorway which led to the adjoining bathroom were *painted* green ivy vines. Along one end, just following the refrigerator which one always bumped upon entering, ran the sink and stove or "the lovely modern kitchenette," as the owner called it with a half-sweep of one hand and a full sweep of the other. At the end of the things that made up the kitchen there was one window which did not open at all. It was sealed shut.

"For your protection," she said, completely discounting air.

Adjoining the sealed window was a door. This did open to the outside on a "patio with definite possibilities." And there *were* "possibilities" of calling a junkman to haul off a ton of stuff and then there were other "possibilities" of shoveling and sweeping for a matter of hours. Over these "possibilities" our only air would move into our little nest.

Through the doorway to the "bath" around which "hung" the painted ivy, one looked up into a pipe-laden ceiling and down at a stained wash-basin ("very expensive at one time and still there because of the war" in 1949), and then if one would see down into the "tub" one first mounted the "throne" which stood easily a foot above the floor level. Seeing down into the tub was better left undone because the tub (also "a war casualty and the complete fault of the government") sloped toward the back instead of toward the drain and in order to empty it completely one had to *push* the water forward for minutes, while straining to keep one's balance from the "throne level," yet still stooping sufficiently to avoid contact with the hot pipes overhead. We eventually knelt while "bailing" the tub.

Passing through the bath to the second "room," the owner scraped her knuckles as she swooped through the rough brick entrance and struck gesture 2B, exclaiming throatily as she swooped:

"Look, isn't this quaint? Genuine brick walls!"

The "old" Gene Price would have let her have it and departed.

The "new" one, sincerely following her wrong "guidance," smiled warmly at the woman, felt genuinely sorry that anyone had to carry on like that, remembered when *she* was almost as obvious, made her Christian witness and said:

"I'll take it. My friend comes in from New York next week. We'll want to move right in."

The "second" room (my office) was a semiconverted coal bin exactly six feet wide and thirteen feet long. Along one end was a closet from whose ceiling a mysterious white powder fell throughout the year. A door that opened out onto the musty, airless, basement hallway had to be locked permanently because there was no room for my big desk otherwise. But even though the owner had developed some type of metaphysical theory that there was no such thing as fresh air, she did consent to have one panel of the door opened onto the old hallway and to install a ventilating fan which pulled nice fresh fuel air in to me from the furnace room next door to my "office."

Now, if you have gone all around the "apartment" with me and found no windows to the outside, you are correct. The health department would never have stood for this, but I was a Christian and Jesus said to turn the other cheek and I did—for Ellen, too, before she had a chance to advance an opinion.

Being a completely impractical extremist and a very, very green Christian, I had absolutely nothing right except my intentions. So, when Ellen arrived she could only do one thing: grow in that Grace she talked about.

This she did. And it was a long, long time before she even let me know how far her heart sank when I first took her gleefully to our "beloved catacombs" where for one year everything financial centered around scraping together one hundred and twenty-five dollars per month for rent.

Considering the way I had lived, and had this been a normal, two-roomed English basement, the rent seemed low enough the day I signed the lease. But I had not reckoned on things being changed quite as much as God had planned to change them.

We moved into the "elegant dungeon" on the first of November, and my first year with Christ began as He began, from the very first crate we unpacked, to transform my first big blunder. Mother had sent us a few lovely things, never dreaming what their setting would be. And although I'm sure she wanted to cry when she realized what was facing her shut up in that dark, airless pocket with a still very carnal and completely unpredictable Christian baby, Ellen laughed and set herself for the *moment* only as she watched Him make transformation number one:

The legs on a lovely walnut chest I was uncrating had been broken in transit.

I *almost* swore as I would have done, drowning the entire laboring class in a torrent of self-satisfied capitalistic phraseology and blaming Roosevelt for everything! Instead, I snapped my fingers, looked up from the broken chest I had just uncrated, and smiled at her.

"Honey, let's get the Lord's picture up on the wall before we call the transit company about this broken leg. They'll send an inspector and I want everybody who comes in our little house to know He lives here with us!"

We hung a copy of Signe Larson's powerful pen drawing of Jesus, read my first chapter of dear old Hannah Smith's *The Christian's Secret of a Happy Life,* had some powdered coffee, beat the dust out of the studio bed our landlady had generously contributed, and on our knees in the midst of crates of books and packing boxes, with the purple rooster watching from the wall above the Lord's picture, we talked to Him for a while and then we went to bed.

*

No decorating was furnished but if we'd get the paint from the hardware store and put it on, the "duchess" would let us deduct the cost of the paint from the rent, and I was so caught up in the wonder of my new life that it all seemed very fair to me. I loved the "duchess" and I loved Ellen and oh, how I loved Christ!

Before I drifted off to sleep that night I had a vague, happy feeling that soon I could like me again, too. At least I felt off my own hands and into His. And in spite of the insane apartment, with my production office gone and no job, I still felt like the daughter of the King, and for the first time in my entire life I knew I was free.

21

Upstairs and Down

It is easier and certainly simpler for an extremist to embark upon a life of Kingdom living. One cannot get along comfortably following Christ unless one is completely willing to be a fool for Him. An extremist is always "completely." In everything.

From having depended upon the Union Club Motor Livery's long, black limousines to deliver me or the merest package for years, I suddenly seemed to forget that even hardware stores deliver. Of course, I owed Union Livery so much money they wouldn't come for me anyway by that time, but had they been willing to go beyond the call of "creditor duty," I had stepped over into another kind of life.

I was free of having to *be* somebody now. I was His child and it was enough. And it was fun to go to the hardware store and carry home paint cans. Somehow it seemed as though I did it for Him. And armed with two new paintbrushes and wearing the whole armor of God, we began to splash white paint upon our pocketbook-brown walls. This was to be just the base coat to blot out some of the dingy brown and to liquidate the rooster and put out the painted yellow candelabra with flames. We cared not one whit whether the brush strokes were even or not, and so we drew big hearts with His name inside them, printed Scripture on the walls and I think for two days the whole thing was fun even for Ellen who is not an extremist.

Her loyal heart and her one hundred pounds labored right along with me and the Everlasting Arms were underneath. And, for two "ten- or eleven-hour" painting days, it *was* fun. But on the third day, when drenched in prayer, I mounted the wobbly ladder to tackle the battery of nine pipes which traversed the entire length of the low cobwebby ceiling, I began to think profoundly upon the chapter in Thomas Kelly called "Entrance Into Suffering."

The muscles in my arms had done no more than support my fingers on the typewriter keys since my dog stopped needing a leash ten years before, and that third day they began to scream in a most Calvinistic fashion! Judging by their behavior the muscles in my forearms were still property of the "old nature," and it must have been alive because they were.

The pipes were three-inch furnace pipes and very hot by eleven in the morning. The fumes made the tears flow and every time my brush rubbed the top of a pipe, flakes of rust fell in my eyes causing more tears to flow.

But, the Lord can *use* everything and he has used the memory of this next moment "at the pipes" to turn desperation to humor a dozen times for me during the past four years. After almost three hours on the ladder in the heat and fumes and falling flakes of rust, the "duchess" descended the stairs from her first-floor luxury, and assuming pose number twenty-six in the doorway of our little dungeon, she swept the ceiling with an outward fling of her plaited leather riding crop and literally *ejaculated*:

"My, but you girls are fortunate! That's the best material available in those lovely pipes. And—isn't it simply marvelous that they all run in the same symmetrical direction?"

For just a moment the ladder wobbled dangerously. Like you, when you read her speech just now, I thought I must be wrong. But that's what she said and Ellen stood there balancing her paint bucket on the corner of a packing box and heard it, too. We were just learning about our friend "upstairs." In fact, we were still learning about her the day we moved. And we were still amazed, although the learning had led to a real fondness by then.

There will be other things to tell you which will be very hard to believe, but this book is definitely not fiction. It is all true. And I am going to be careful not to over-batter your ability to believe. But while we're on the subject of the "duchess" and the pipes, I feel tempted to add that she suggested also, just before she ascended the stairs again that day, that we might hang artificial Spanish moss over the already dust-caked pipes for an unusual "touch of decor."

I had truly been born again. I was tremendously excited about my new Christian life. I had no intention whatever of going back. But had Spanish moss somehow found its way into that "whited sepulchre," things might have been very different for us both today.

What did we do after she left besides pat and soothe our screaming, twitching muscles?

We did what we have done for four years and more now.

We looked at Him and laughed.

The "duchess" and her pipes "of the very best material, all running the same symmetrical direction" did more than any other single thing to throw us safely over into the Holy hilarity of God where His really happy saints live and laugh.

*

Our friend, whom we nicknamed the "duchess" because "Mrs." was so inadequate, was as kind as her wealth would allow her to be. She liked us and we really liked her. In her magnificent living room "upstairs" sat a "magnificent" Mason-Hamlin grand piano with a tone like the music Bach must have heard when he wrote. And our friend the landlady offered to allow Ellen to practice on it every day while she was off riding one of her three horses, which she did every morning at ten-thirty.

We thanked Him from the depths of our hearts for this because it seemed so wrong for Ellen to be far from a piano for long. She and the Mason-Hamlin sat right over my head when I sat in my converted coal-bin "office," but since I was converted, too, I trained myself to write and concentrate under varying rhythms and pedal thumpings.

And during these times when Ellen was "upstairs" He was very close to me. So was His enemy some days, and one morning I remember sharply. The desire to feel the dark "escape" of a North Side bar at midmorning rushed over me as I sat "penned" in the space behind my desk in my "office" with the ventilating fan to the furnace room and the "genuine brick walls." I got up to fly out the basement front door by the garbage cans, "our entrance," before Ellen came back "downstairs." But as I stood up Ellen began to play my special song upstairs. Like the Lord's Own Tears, the gentle, minor-key music came floating "downstairs" to haunt and hold me to His side.

> Into the woods my Master went,
> Clean, forspent, forspent;
> Into the woods my Master came,
> Forspent with love and shame.
>
> But the olives they were not blind to Him,
> The little gray leaves were kind to Him,
> The thorn-tree had a mind to Him,
> When into the woods He came.

Sidney Lanier's "little gray leaves" being kind to Him always melted me. And when Ellen began to play it through again, more strongly this time, I fell on my knees by my damask-cushioned vanity stool where I prayed alone, and wept and wept and wept at what I had almost done. This was not the last time I wept for the same or similar reasons. And the elegant damask stool looked less and less out of place with the tear stains marking the ever-filtering coal dust in my converted "office" with its genuine brick walls and the Presence in the midst.

22

No Room for Dramatics!

The most I had to contribute to our establishment in a material way Mother and Dad had given me—the first month's rent, the moving bill, and some of our furniture. Having closed my office abruptly, I walked out of it loaded with debts. They didn't seem so bad to me because I had had them around for a long time, but I could see Ellen steady herself when I looked up from a pile of past due bills and said:

"Oh, yeah . . . here's another one I'd forgotten. One hundred and forty dollars to Union Livery for my June, July and August service."

"What's that one that fell on the floor, Genie?"

"Oh, let me see. Oh, yeah—Adolph? This is one I thought I wouldn't bring up right away."

"Liquor bill?"

"Some drugs, too, and magazines and he used to cash my checks so I could pay Marie, my maid, every Friday. I probably 'charged' a few of those checks, too."

"How much is it all together?" She was very careful with me at times like this.

"How much is it? Really want to know?" I smiled what was definitely not a saintly smile because I didn't yet know how to handle things entirely without tricks. "Really want to know?"

"Yes. We'll have to begin to pay it."

"Oh—uh, yeah. Sure. Well, it's four hundred and fifty-six dollars and ninety-three cents."

At that moment our "front" door buzzer sounded off and I nearly went with it. It hadn't rung before and I had a return of my old panic at doorbells with no one to protect me from collectors and people I didn't want to see.

"What do you think that could mean?" My chest hurt. "Could we just let it ring?"

"Christians don't have any right to let their doorbells ring. Maybe it's someone in trouble."

"Oh, I forgot. I'm sorry. I'll go myself."

On the way to the door I asked the Lord to forgive me for wanting to let it ring. But when I saw who it was, I knocked over the "duchess" dress form standing guard over some old furniture in the basement hall in my flight back to Ellen and safety.

"What'll I do? It's the news agency from my old place. They've found me. I owe them money."

"Well, first of all, we'll let him in, and then we'll give him ten dollars on account and tell him things are going to be different from now on."

"Ten dollars! He wouldn't accept such a little bit, would he?"

"Let's tell him about you and see what happens."

I told him about me and he took the ten dollars and was very polite about taking all the rest in two- and five-dollar payments over a period of months. And down the long list of creditors we went. Some I called by telephone, some I visited in person. To others I wrote letters. But to each one I told the complete truth. I had become a Christian. They would get the money.

"If you trusted me when I was drinking all that Scotch," I said to my friend at the drugstore on Chicago Avenue, "then it seems a good idea to trust me now because Jesus Christ is handling my checkbook as well as me from now on."

Month after month two-dollar payments went out on my top-heavy debts. Two dollars. Two dollars. Two dollars. And much later, after every creditor had graciously accepted the appallingly small but very regular payments, I found out that two dollars is the minimum amount which a creditor can accept and not sue.

I didn't know that, but the Holy Spirit did.

*

Now, periodically in my life, I had made excellent money. Continually, I expected to. Winter 1949 was no different in my expectation department, although I wasn't too sure how to go about it. Having had my own production office for five years I was out of things contact-wise on the free-lance writer's market. I had been the top writer in the Chicago files of the Music Corporation of America, the country's biggest talent agency, and so thought naturally I would be able to write my own ticket when I decided to go out looking for a writing job again. The thing that puzzled me was that I was not the slightest bit interested in radio anymore!

"I still have a little money left, Genie, let's be sure what He wants you to do. Don't rush ahead of the Holy Spirit."

I meant to spin around like an executive in my swivel chair before my desk in my "converted office" and bumped my knee sharply on the corner of a drawer instead. We both laughed. My impatience and my oversupply of dramatics were taking a redemptive beating.

Instead of spinning like an executive, I just shoved back and crawled out. There was literally *no room* for melodramatics in my life now. When I wanted to pace, it had to be up and down because of the six feet of width.

"The Lord seems to be telling me *not* to ask Mother and Dad for a cent."

"Oh, that's wonderful. You're making real progress now."

"I am?" Nothing pleased me at all anymore except for someone to see that I was growing a little as a Christian.

"Yes, you are. Do you know why He's telling you not to ask them?"

"I think so. Because I've always depended on them in the tight places. He wants me to depend solely upon Him now. Also He wants Mother and Dad to see that I'm depending on God and not on them as I've always done. They've grown away from Him because of me. He wants them back, too. I've got to let them see He's really changed me." We both smiled before I said this: "And nothing would prove to Mother and Dad that I'm a *new creature* like no collect telegrams for money!"

Ellen reached for *The Christian's Secret of a Happy Life*.

"This is today. We're both willing to do exactly what He wants us to do. Right now it's time we began to read. Be too cold in here even for you to sit up after a while!"

She handed the book to me and jumped into bed to keep warm. We had the furnace itself practically in our laps, but the heat went "upstairs." It was chilly going but not once did it occur to us to neglect our times with Him. Quite without our planning it, the days seemed to divide themselves into almost regular "sessions."

Morning Bible reading and prayer. And then quiet before Him, during which time I was gradually able to sit still and actually think about Christ for five to ten minutes at a time.

After that more good reading . . . Thomas à Kempis, F. B. Meyer, Henry Drummond, Andrew Murray, Brother Lawrence, C. S. Lewis, the pungencies of Oswald Chambers, and many other saints of God who shared their wonder with us in our little "whited sepulchre" as we read aloud hour after hour from the books they had written.

Prayer, Bible study, reading the saints, silence, intercession in the afternoon, and then the one Light-filled night when, on our knees side by side we made a permanent and complete surrender of every right to ourselves into the hands of the living Christ.

We stepped forever—as far as we can see—into His glorious captivity. Into freedom. Without the load of our "rights." Indeed, the Burden *was* Light.

And every winter Sunday morning we dressed up in our good suits which did not match our dungeon, and with Ellen wearing a borrowed mink coat on *top* of her own inadequate winter coat, we stepped joyfully around the corner to church with the very elite.

I now wanted to go to church. And wisely Ellen agreed to let me choose. My main qualification was a church where I'd be left alone. Where no one would try to shake my hand and make me feel "welcome." For some reason I loved people everywhere except in church!

Oswald Chambers says "individuality is all elbows." It is. I should know. But I was still elbowing my way through some of the time. And church with our elite and weary neighbors right around the elegant corner suited me exactly. They were not interested in me and I was not interested in them. This was not altogether Christian but it was the case.

Everyone seemed so interested in himself that only Ellen and I knew her mink coat was borrowed and much too long, and we thought at least that we were the only ones who knew we could afford no more than ten cents apiece in the collection plate. Of course we knew He knew, but He also knew this was really what we had to drop in. Ellen's reserve was running low.

And once a week we needed thirteen cents each for bus fare to get to a prayer group where I experienced my first informal Christian fellowship and found it increasingly attractive.

A few people came to call on us. Only four ever came back the second time and two were drinking. And our Holy hilarity increased each time some unsuspecting person dropped by or responded innocently to an invitation from us, because waiting for the looks on their faces when first they glimpsed our "whited sepulchre" came to be our favorite amusement.

And it was so inexpensive.

We asked the three women who had befriended me right after my conversion to have tea one afternoon. They came very properly and very promptly with flowers. And they endeared themselves to us permanently because they actually sat balancing Mother's lovely Chinese Seasons teacups and discussed further decoration of our basement abode! These three ladies are real ladies. And all their careful home-training showed that day. No one laughed until I couldn't endure not laughing one more minute. And this happened when I was standing on my bed elaborately demonstrating where we would hang the equally elaborate, carved gold sconces poor unsuspecting Mother had just sent!

We all knew they'd never be hung in the "sepulchre"—neither the sconces nor the walnut Chippendale mirror nor the Italian miniatures. The lovely china Victorian lamp with the yellow roses and silk shade looked ridiculous enough against the streaked white walls. And we had long since decided one coat on the "duchess'" walls more than took care of the "second mile." Also with the "second mile" in mind we reported nothing to the OPA. In fact, we rejoiced because our wealthy landlady kept us well exercised on the "second mile" and pink of cheek with the perpetual turning of the other.

We left the walls with the chalky base coat and this, too, had its spiritual advantages. Because on the wall over Ellen's daybed stood a white brushstroke named Paul and over my bed another (a bit less stern) whose name came to be John. There were also milk bottles, two quarts and one pint, on three snow-covered back steps along the wall where the rooster had been, and on the wall behind the record player a plump lady in a ballet skirt stood the entire year on one toe. The ballet lady had spiritual significance, too, because she made us remember the wonderful line from Henry Drummond which describes the Christian who pirouettes through life on a single text!

We enjoyed our "whited" figures on the walls of our cheerful dungeon and they gave us a reason to rejoice at no windows. If we had had windows and less wall we might not have had the ballet lady, or John or Paul or the milk bottles on the back steps.

And even when we used our last ten dollars to get an old friend of mine out of a jam, we rejoiced because He had long since proven to us beyond the shadow of any doubt that He meant it literally when He said, "My burden is light."

23

Kingdom Work

We did use our last ten dollars to help a friend of mine who was not a Christian. To keep me solvent, we had put Ellen's savings in my account and the balance showed twelve in the bank. I wrote a check for ten, leaving the required two to keep the account open. My old friend, already convinced I was insane, seemed impressed when the next morning's mail brought the ten dollars back in a letter filled with love from the Greenlees back home. They are relatives who interested me not one bit through the years because they remained Christians and prayed for the Prices. Of course, at my conversion these dear, gentle people and my cousin Pearl, a blond saint, who married a minister, were the first I wanted to see. In spite of the way I had treated all of them, they were happy to see me and opened their arms and I saw that their hearts had never been closed to me as mine had been to them.

The Greenlees taught me the great spiritual lesson of being able to receive when they began sending us ten-dollar checks out of their tithe money.

Ellen tried valiantly to get a job.

I made the rounds of the advertising agencies and networks. A few years before, some of the men I visited had offered me good fees just to write audition material. I wrote some sample scripts for a show I wouldn't have touched out of my own office and I worked hard on them. But they were flatly rejected!

There was no reason given. The agency just couldn't use them.

Ellen's money was gone one day. I hadn't had any for several weeks, but we had our guidance clear about not asking our families for help. In fact, that never crossed our minds. We were not remotely worried, we were just waiting. And the closed doors were messages from Him to wait a little longer.

Neither of us was trained for practical earning. Ellen's training was advanced, but it was in classical piano. All I could do was write and direct radio scripts. No one seemed to need anything played or written for money. And yet we knew He meant every word He said when He said that we were to seek the Kingdom first and all we needed would be added unto us.

The Lord had walked right up to Ellen in the person of the strange little old man in the New York church almost five years before and told her that we were to depend directly upon His promise. Our part was to seek the Kingdom first.

And we had been doing that.

And one late afternoon when the "duchess' " third janitor in ten days had departed in a rage, an idea hit me. Ellen was out following up a not too likely ad in the paper and I could scarcely wait for her to come home. And when I heard our buzzer vibrating the building with her customary "three shorts," I was halfway down the low-ceilinged hallway before she got the key unstuck in the lock of our basement "front door."

"Hey, I've a terrific idea!"

"I didn't get the job."

"Good. Now listen!"

I began to whisper so our friend "upstairs" wouldn't hear. After all, there was no insulation on our ceiling. Just those splendid pipes of the best material all running the same way, and then her floor boards were there.

I explained that janitor number three had just departed in a cloud of invectives and justifiable fury. We knew it was *humanly impossible* to satisfy the poor woman but I figured it be *super*-humanly *possible*.

"So, let's you and I apply for the jobs! She's lost her maid, too. Between us we can be maid and janitor and grow spiritually, keep both cheeks pink from turning and I'll lose weight while we're both going the *sixty*-second mile! It'll be a wonderful chance to prove our Christianity is working, and she should give us at least half, if not two-thirds, off on our rent! Maybe she'd even allow a hundred dollars for the services of two people. That would only leave twenty-five a month and I can knock out *something somebody* will buy eventually!"

I knew her answer long before I finished my excited tirade. Ellen was remembering the tight-mouthed, cynical, proud, boasting woman who regaled her just a few months before with rave notices about Eugenia Price Productions.

Here was the same girl excited about the possibility of emptying garbage and scrubbing floors!

Ellen didn't rave. I am the raver. She just stood there with her slanty eyes brimming with happy tears and said:

"Behold I make all things new!"

"Who said that?"

"Jesus."

"Isn't He wonderful? Let's go ask her!"

This was almost too much for the strange woman "upstairs." She paced up and down the long, long living room in her riding habit for several moments and then whirled upon us with:

"But you're both ladies! You can't do servants' work!"

"Jesus Christ did." I said that.

She said nothing for a moment.

"We want to do this for you. We know you're in a spot and so are we. We haven't any money to continue paying this rent every month. Two months ago we pooled our Christmas money from our families to pay you. Last month I sold a coat Mother had just given me. This month we'll work for you if you'll let us. It won't bother us. It really won't. We're free."

She turned away so neither of us could see the effect my words had on her, but in a moment she whirled back:

"All right, it sounds like a gay lark! If you'll look at it as a lark and a favor to me, and not as though I'm hiring you as my servants, I'll agree."

We thanked Him silently and rejoiced as we rubbed one cheek. Then she graciously added:

"I'll knock off *thirty* dollars a month from your rent, too!"

A moment later, descending the stairs to our cheerful dungeon, we each rubbed the other cheek and rejoiced some more. For two hours a day, six days a week, I would carry garbage and scrub halls and porch and sweep the sidewalk and keep the yard clean and planted. For two hours a day, six days a week, Ellen would work in the "duchess'" apartment. And we would each be making the equivalent of fifteen dollars per month!

We still had ninety-five dollars a month rent to raise, but we had the Lord and He had us and that night as we read the chapter on "Growth" in dear Hannah Whitall Smith's *The Christian's Secret of a Happy Life*, we could actually feel ourselves grow.

Ellen's job changed abruptly after the first day. She was fired as a domestic in no uncertain terms! Not for any inadequacy on her part, but because our landlady couldn't stand to *watch* a lady work. I was outside in the halls and yard so she didn't have to *see* me.

"It's more than I can bear, Ellen! You'll just have to stop."

"But we need to make this money, and your apartment is so beautiful I don't mind at all. Everything in here is like dusting a museum piece!"

"Nevertheless *I* can't bear it another day. From now on you will accompany me while I sing!"

As a Christian I can say no more than that the woman no doubt could sing once, but there had been an accident. And so Ellen's work was *really* difficult after that. The voice and the knowledge of singing had been there once. The knowledge of singing was still there. But even though almost every day the eccentric, lonely, and strangely lovable woman would call "downstairs":

"Girls! My voice is coming through—listen!"—it never really came.

But Ellen went on accompanying. Day after day, if my garbage chores were finished, I'd sit "downstairs" in my converted coal bin and pray as they struggled through "Vienna Life" and the "Kashmiri Love Song."

And then *"it"* would begin. And if you will turn back mentally or literally to Part One of this book, to the page on "Malagueña," the flowery Spanish number which Ellen made sound like marvelous music, you will know what I mean by "it."

"Malagueña" struck the "duchess'" fancy; day after day after the songs were ended, the "creative exercises" began as she thumped

and stretched and beat the floor in rhythm to the beat of "Malagueña."
It was not dancing. It was as nearly as I could see from having been
called up to watch several times, just what she called it—"creative
exercises." And after "Malagueña" while Ellen ate cottage cheese
and fruit with her, or brushed the "duchess'" hair, depending upon
her mood, they talked about God. Her conception of God was her
own. And it somewhat described a liberal Baptist coming out of a
Hindu temple with a rosary around her neck and a copy of Mary
Baker Eddy under her arm.

An "advanced form of metaphysics" she called it.

And each day we grew to love the woman more and although she
didn't say so, we believe she came to see that Jesus Christ hung on
a very real Cross for her sins as well as ours. She said there was no
"material" at all. This did not include our monthly check, however.
But one day she swept across her thick living room oriental (with a
gesture, of course) and declared:

"Now, that rug means nothing to me. It is just the *idea* of the
rug that I love!"

Ellen moved right in and said: *"I* think you love that rug."

The "duchess" laughed loudly and forgot her diction for a moment.

"You're doggone right. I do!"

*

No regular job for which we were qualified ever turned up during
the first six months of the lease. "My father worketh hitherto and I
work." My Father was working "to will and to do of his good
pleasure." He had tried Ellen in New York and now was taking her
deeper. Obviously He was trying me.

We both longed to "dwell deep." And deeper.

"Every time we obey Him on the tiniest thing, Genie, He transforms
us on that point and it becomes a permanent part of our personalities.
You'll be free of ever minding being a servant for the rest of your
life. So will I. But I'm so really proud of you, dear heart, because
you're going all the way with Him and you're such a baby in Christ.
Matter of fact, it keeps me hopping to stay up with you!"

Where was He taking us?

We didn't bother to wonder. After all, Jesus Himself said that we should "take no thought for the morrow: for the morrow shall take thought for the things of itself."

I have always taken Him very literally. Everything He said.

And day by day the burden grew lighter and lighter. I never felt the Presence of Jesus Christ more definitely than in the dark alcove under the front steps when I stooped to spread rat poison on pieces of stale bread to discourage a sudden pilgrimage of fat gray friends as they sought to inhabit the big oil drums where I daily dumped the "upstairs" people's waste and garbage. Christ knelt there in the shadows with me and one day I had to remain very quiet because five large rats, one following the other, came up right above my head as I stooped to pick up a couple of empty brandy bottles and a bread wrapper I had dropped. And then they all went down the side of the wall in silent procession. I am not a squeamish female, but neither am I attracted to rats. But He was there and I was His and my heart didn't even pick up speed.

"Lo, I am with you always," even in the shadows by the garbage cans.

24

The Glop-Era Begins to End

If you are interested in "glop" I am sure Ellen will send you her recipe. Then you take it from there because that's what we did night after night. It begins with rice *and* . . . . And on it goes. On our "glop" went until one Friday it found itself consisting of noodles and canned beef and a touch of rice and bacon with a suggestion of tomato after it had begun on Monday with rice and bacon and a whole can of tomatoes. Two bay leaves added on Wednesday did something for it and for us.

Looking back on these lean but starchy days of pure paradox we could both have shouted then and will shout now:

"The more 'glop' the more Glory and the more Glory the more 'glop'!"

We would have meant it then and we mean it now.

Month after month for six of them we got by gloriously and gracefully. We were fully supplied with both Glory and Grace and just enough money came in dribbles as we took care of a couple of sick friends along with other odd jobs to supplement our janitor service and Ellen's accompanying. Of course, when her maid-service career ended in one day, Ellen joined me with the vacuum in the long halls and up and down the wide-carpeted "upstairs" stairways, with the broom and hose on the sidewalks, the rake and hoe in the yards front and back. I also did some typing for an old friend who had her own business. She used to borrow money from me in the old days and never in her wildest moments expected Gene Price to be "her girl" as she spoke of me on the telephone with her business associates. I loved it, though, and I loved her more than I had ever loved her and we had been good friends for a long, long time. Ellen answered her telephone for a regular number of hours a day, too, for a while and we both thank her so much for everything now.

`Especially for the elegant steak dinners and the expensive and delectable delicatessen spreads she and another friend laid before us on occasion.

The three friends who entertained me after my conversion until I could find an apartment also had us out to their home on the south side often in those dear "glop-days." We sang all the way out on the "L" and all the way back because we knew they were terrific cooks and always made up a surprise box for us to bring home. Having known me in my other life, they all hesitated to hand us a five-dollar bill. They thought they were making it easier to do it by invitations and in boxes. We love them all for it all and now that we can have steaks or rare rib roasts for dinner, we don't enjoy any of it as we did the "dinner" we prepared out of one of these gift boxes from our friends. The menu that night consisted of cake mix baked in a muffin pan, with bacon, and a hot dish of canned carrots on the side. And we thanked Him. Oh, how we thanked Him.

And as I write this, I realize with shame that our thanks for our abundance now does not come from as deep in our hearts as it did in the entirely Blessed Glop-Era.

During this first six-month period, Ellen had another compelling as strong as the one that sent her to Chicago to be with me. This one was to teach herself to type. Naturally, she couldn't go to school to learn and so being as she is, she simply called the Smith-Corona people and asked them to send her a book.

They did and sometimes to my annoyance she pecked away at my old Corona hour after hour until she became what she is now, a good typist and of course, very accurate. Later on, you will see where this "compelling" followed the plan.

*

Day continued to follow day and on one of them I had lunch with Shep Chartoc, who was my agent when MCA owned me five years before. Shep was a wonderful agent and an even better friend, and he was thrilled when I told him about what Jesus Christ had done in my life. I told him how the doors to work which we both knew would have opened a few months before had closed now. I also told him that more and more I was beginning to think God was calling me into some kind of work for Him. But there was just nothing for an experienced writer of radio drama in Gospel broadcasting. I told him what Ellen had said about this and he smiled with me. You see, when I remarked to her one day that I'd never be able to use my daytime serial experience for Christ because sponsors are afraid of the mention of the Cross, she said:

"Christ knows a lot more about radio even than you know, Genie." She had jumped into deep water so often by then, she could almost swim in it.

We both thought her naïve about the "business."

Shep and I talked some more and when I rummaged through my purse for a pencil to make a note of something as we were ready to leave, I came suddenly upon a tiny, quite forgotten yellow envelope which I had carried for over a year.

It contained enough sleeping pills to take my own life. Shep and I crumbled them all up in the ashtray on the table and in a few minutes he was able to laugh about it, too. He had known me and had seen me often during that year and this was quite a surprise to him.

The next day the program director of a new Catholic FM station called and asked me to take over an hour and a half record show, five days a week, beamed at shut-ins. It seems my dear friend Shep had convinced him that I had "religion" now and would work for the very nominal FM religious station salary. Ellen and I put it in the Lord's hands and I went for the interview. I had never been before a microphone myself in my life. My spot was always behind the control room window. This didn't seem to matter to them and without any doubt whatever, Ellen and I felt I should take the job.

The "duchess" had FM on her radio and she and Ellen listened every morning from nine to ten-thirty to "A Visit with Genie." And for the same basic reason she had fired Ellen as her maid, she fired me as her janitor.

"I just can't tolerate the embarrassment of having her come home from the radio station as she does each day and begin to carry garbage! What would my neighbors think anyway?"

I felt a little disappointed when I received my dismissal. I really didn't mind the garbage routine at all by then but she agreed to continue to give us the apartment for the "moderate" ninety-dollar figure. Instead of singing "My God and I" as I squirted the hose on her dusty sidewalks, I sang it as He and I stepped happily along the same sidewalks to work at the radio station every morning at eight-fifteen.

For the first week I sounded like "Kawliga" the wooden Indian, but gradually I discarded my carefully written out scripts and began to have a marvelous time adlibbing about everything from Persian pottery to birthstones and played music from Bach to "barber shop," but carefully checking it all with the Lord first in the record library every morning in prayer. More than once He prompted me to replace a recording I had selected because it was not on His level. And this close intimacy with Him among the records each morning intrigued my listeners and helped lessen the agony of soul I endured some nights as I knelt by my bed to pray. In the back basement apartment (all completely finished!) lived the jazz music critic of one of the big magazines. The music he loved had been like my blood for years and some nights the pull back was painful and I could only kneel there and let it beat on me and know Christ knelt with me with healing in His hand.

He "worked" through my record show each morning with me and each time He would tell me not to use a record I'd report to my fanatically loyal listeners that our guest of honor had made the suggestion that I change a record. My fan mail came flowing in and soon surpassed all the other programs combined. My listeners loved my personal relationship with Christ.

I was not a Catholic, and several times innocently programmed what turned out to be Protestant hymns until someone who knew the difference happened to hear. The recordings were all about Jesus Christ and the mistake was unintentional. I apologized and one of the women on the regular staff who was a Catholic kindly offered to monitor me from that time on.

Everyone was gracious to me and I believe I made some enduring friendships there. Friendships that will go right on through eternity.

Within three or four months it was suggested that I should begin an afternoon "Visit with Genie." I used to tape record my afternoon quarter hour while a twenty-minute classical recording whirled away for the pleasure of my shut-in listeners on the morning "Visit with Genie."

Ellen did my research and by the middle of September, 1950, I was restless for more work to do. The station had raised my salary once and another raise was volunteered, but I wanted to write again. The first month after my conversion I talked constantly of the "great Christian novel" I would write. Ellen, through the Holy Spirit, knew I was *not* ready spiritually. And it was then I learned that He wanted *me* first, and my talent just went along with me the way my hands and my feet went. Not necessarily first.

But in September of 1950 I felt that old stirring within. I hadn't written anything but letters for over a year. I felt I had something to say and I tossed in the night under the influence of strong, rhythmic phrases and brilliant descriptive passages which I lost completely upon waking.

I wanted so much to write *something* again.

But what? I prayed for guidance.

"Are you willing *not* to write at all—ever again, if that's the plan, Genie?"

"You know I am. But I love you for pinning me down. I'm really not cooking anything up this time, Ellen. Somehow this *seems* different." I laughed. "Of course, that could be wishful thinking."

It could have been. But it so happened this time it was not. It was prayer about to be answered. Prayers from two sources. Ours and one other. And once the answer was set in motion it really moved. Sometime during the third week in September an advertising man named John Camp called me on the telephone. He said he owned the J. M. Camp advertising agency with headquarters in Fort Wayne, Indiana, and he asked if I would meet him in the lobby of a Loop hotel that afternoon on an urgent matter.

I met him and for the first time in my life I heard of the Pacific Garden Mission. For four years, Mr. Harry Saulnier, Superintendent of the old Skid Row Mission and his board of Christian businessmen, had been praying for guidance concerning a possible half-hour dramatic program telling true stories of the lives which had been transformed by Jesus Christ at the Pacific Garden Mission. They had the stories, they had purchased the time on radio station WGN, but there was a missing piece in the picture. They needed a writer-producer with both professional and Christian experience.

My writer-heart leaped with delight, but I didn't trust the "writer" in me and Mr. Camp agreed to give me a day in which to seek the Lord's Will for *me* in the unique radio venture. We prayed and waited for His answer. It came with full assurance. And on the first Saturday night in October, 1950, I directed my first broadcast of the now world-famous radio program "Unshackled!"

The first three scripts were written in my converted coal bin as the Blessed Glop-Era in the dungeon ended. As though to mark it well, a thunderstorm flooded Chicago and our inadequate plumbing proved itself most inadequate. In fact, there was "nothing comparable" to the feeling we shared as we sat one night discussing an "Unshackled" script when lo, the rains came inside and spread an inch of water over the dungeon floor.

There was a tinge of kindly retribution, because that night *we* slept "upstairs"! On the third floor in the most beautiful apartment of all, on the "duchess' " orchid sheets!

The next day and for the entire week thereafter, large eager water bugs moved in, but we had had those orchid sheets and had slept "upstairs" one night and our time had come to go anyway.

On October fifteenth we left our "whited sepulchre" to the bugs and our love and our gratitude with our friend "upstairs."

The gratitude we left with her is deeper and more and different from that which anyone casual might suspect. And from our hearts we hope the year lightened her life a bit. It was certainly used of God to sharpen our souls *and* our humors.

And it deepened our hearts.

I had skimmed in scampering across the surface of my new life. After Ellen had gone with the movers, I swept out the little dungeon for the last time "dwelling deep" in the riches in Glory.

25

Across Cornell Avenue

It is interesting to me that the apartment which the Lord had waiting for us not only filled our needs for a combined home and office, fitted our income and had the added glory of a wood-burning fireplace, but its location made silent witness to what the Lord *knew* He had accomplished in my life already. Out of the "catacombs" He set me back down just across Cornell Avenue from where I had lived ten years before when I found "near Reality." I believe He kept me "Near North" until I met the hedonism of my old life in the Power of my new life, and then back He sent me to Cornell Avenue where I had a chance to meet the old intellectual retreatism with the infinitely Higher Call of the new.

There were times when *I* was not at all sure, but I didn't need to be sure, because *God* knew He had spoiled everything unlike Himself for me by then. He knew the call of the extravagant life of excess went headfirst into the big oil drums along with the upstairs garbage during the first year in the Kingdom School. He knew I would never again deceive nor depend upon my parents instead of Him. The easier-to-break, obvious ties and habits were broken. Writing had been completely surrendered and ambition swept into the gutter as surely as though I had pushed it there with my big janitor's broom.

The would-be "little big-shot" now *wanted* only to be His.

And on Cornell Avenue the second time, with Ellen all changed over from the A & P to the Jewel Food Store, He began to probe us both more deeply; at the same time daring to trust Himself to carry on His work on "Unshackled" through this thirteen-month-old Kingdom beginner. The year of the Glop-Era in the "beloved catacombs" may seem to have been wasted. My old friends certainly considered it pathetic. But the hour after hour during day after day we spent in study and reading from the Word of God had carved deeply into my very being. And although the writing of a true story ending with a conversion scene each week is a script assignment from which anyone in his right mind would run, I confess I was not afraid of it. Just before it came my way, Ellen and I had spent time in the fifteenth chapter of the Gospel of John, and I was absolutely convinced that as long as I stayed hooked onto the Vine, the scripts would be *poured through me like sap*.

He was a God of His Word, wasn't He?

The only condition involved in His constant supply to His branches is staying in contact with Him. But this requires faith. Faith holds us to the Vine, and after I had written "Unshackled" for a month or so, one day a fear came, my faith trembled and the typewriter stopped clicking.

Ellen heard the silence for half an hour or so, and then I heard her footsteps in the long hall connecting her "living-room office and bedroom" with my room.

She sat down on the big old wooden rocker in which my Grandmother Price had rocked both my Dad and me when we were babies.

"Want to talk about it?"

"Yes. What really happened to me when I was born again?"

"Do you doubt that something *did* happen, Genie?"

I got up impatiently.

"No! No, that's not the point. I know something happened! I wouldn't be sitting here writing a big half-hour radio show for a Skid Row Mission if something hadn't happened! But what I want to know is how in the name of common sense am I going to explain it every week on 'Unshackled'? Do you realize I have to write a conversion scene every week on this thing? I think the windup is the most important part of the show and I'm the one who's stuck with explaining it! To pagans and atheists and agnostics and skeptics and Buddhists and—how in the name of common sense am I going to do it?"

She looked as helpless as I felt.

"I'm sure I don't know, but I don't think you can do it 'in the name of common sense.' It's too hard! Remember what we said yesterday? 'If common sense had been enough, Christ would not have needed to die.' "

"I know you're right. I don't mean to be complaining. I'm just scared! I don't want to use a lot of theological-sounding phrases because I want people who are just as ignorant of the Bible and redemption as I was to understand what I'm saying!"

"You've written five conversion scenes. They were wonderful."

"But this thing might go on for a long, long time! And so far the people whose stories I'm telling remember everything except their conversion scene. They're no help at all."

"I wish I could remember more about mine."

"I know, I know. It isn't a matter of the mind. It's a matter of the spirit. Our spirit and His Spirit." Then an idea hit me. "Hey, let's pretend we have someone here listening who doesn't understand a thing about it. Someone who sits there and raises an eyebrow at me and says: "So what? You say you're a Christian, you say you were converted in a hotel room in New York City, but that doesn't tell me a thing about myself and Christ. What are you really saying? How did He really *get you*? What really happened?"

Ellen looked out the window at the ugly "second" bricks on the side of the apartment building just across a four-foot areaway. And then she said:

"Well, first of all, you had to recognize that life does not end here. That there is a God, that Jesus Christ is God's one revelation of Himself . . . that God came to earth in the Person of Jesus of Nazareth."

"That 'God was in Christ reconciling the world unto Himself.' "

I beamed with delight as I always did and still do when I am able to quote a verse exactly.

Ellen went on. "That God Himself hung on the Cross in the person of Jesus and shed His own blood. God's own heart broke open on the Cross and His Love poured out. And somehow, by a mystery we can't understand, we are justified with the Father, the minute we *believe* what Christ did for us on that Cross! Believe what He did and *receive* Him as our Saviour."

"Now, wait a minute, hold it. That's all true. But that word *justified* is too theological. Could I just say, when we believe Christ died for us on the Cross, we are automatically given a clean slate with the Father? We're made one with Him because Christ stretched Himself over the gap between us and the Father?''

"Certainly. Same thing. And it's much clearer to me that way. What He did I guess was smother our sin in His own heart.''

"That's what gives the peace, isn't it? 'The peace that passeth all understanding.' But there's so much more. That's what gets me tied up in knots when I try to write it down. There isn't time to tell it all every week.''

"I suppose you'll just have to put the emphasis on the particular point which caused the trouble in that person's life. And I believe the Holy Spirit will give you a fresh way to explain everyone's *need* for conversion each week.''

"And if He does that, He'll have to give me the right verses and words to explain how it's done, won't He? Actually, it's the simplest transaction in the world, isn't it? In that hotel room a year ago I just began to agree with God! I began to—believe that what the Bible said is right, after all. And that meant being willing to turn away from my old life to follow Christ into a brand new life.''

"If everyone who turns would make as definite and as complete a break with the old life as you did, Genie, you'd never run out of stories.''

"That's really all we have to do, isn't it? Turn and begin to follow Him. He had been following me all those years. Now I'm following Him. I changed places with God. He's God in my life now. I resigned. What a relief to agree with God. 'Believe on the Lord Jesus Christ and thou shalt be saved.' '' I smiled. "I think that word *saved* is overused and limited, but I like it now. I *was* saved, when I believed, wasn't I?''

"I think you should make it clear always on 'Unshackled' that *believe* means to commit. Not just intellectual belief that Jesus Christ is the Son of God. We can believe it and still not be willing to let Him change us one bit. That was my trouble for so many years.''

I was writing Ben Engstrom's story on "Unshackled" that day.

Ben, who is now one of my favorite people and a very dear friend, was a man embarked on a restless search. He lost his excellent positions at the big steel mills near Chicago because his search took him, ultimately, to the bottle. On Skid Row, through Superintendent Harry Saulnier in a street meeting, Christ reached down and ended dear Ben's long years of searching. Ben tried baseball, show business, success in his work, and the bottle. Nothing fit the empty space in his life except the Person of Jesus Christ. Ben took Jesus Christ literally. He became as a little child and believed. He depends on nothing and no one outside of the Person of his Lord. No wonder Ben and I are fast friends. Our search is over. We have been found.

My fear and nervousness over the long weeks of conversion scenes that stretched ahead vanished, too. I felt ashamed when I remembered what Jesus Himself had said: "Lo, I am with you alway."

He said it again to me that day. "Lo, I am with you alway . . . and I will be even unto the end of 'Unshackled.' "

"Unshackled" has been on the air for three and one half years, summer and winter, as I write these lines and I am more than "absolutely convinced" that Jesus was telling the truth about the things that happen Vine-wise and branch-wise. Not once has this "branch" had to plead with the Vine to send down more sap! On a commercial program of the nature of "Unshackled," there would be at least two and perhaps three writers, a director and a producer. Someone asked me not long ago about the size of my "staff."

I replied: "There are four. The Trinity and Genie Price."

I should have said five, because if Ellen forgot even for one day to take care of *everything* else, including me, I'd never make the regular deadlines of scripts, books and speaking dates.

Her "compelling" to teach herself to type, was of course, a direct "leading" as the Quakers say. Because by winter of 1951, the correspondence required to arrange my speaking dates and to answer my personal "Unshackled" mail was a fulltime job for one person. But there again was a staff of four. The Trinity and Ellen.

26

Given and Taken Away and Given

I was still on the air twice a day with my morning and afternoon "Visits with Genie" and with the combined salaries from "Unshackled" and the "Visits," we expected to fare quite evenly and be able to cut down my debts some each month. Be it remembered that Christian salaries are Christian salaries and we needed them both to make ends meet after the move.

We actually felt flushed enough to invest the staggering sum of seventy-five dollars in an amazingly tall, rebuilt upright piano. A monster designed in the era when piano manufacturers hated piano movers. It must have been lined with granite; surely it was striped oak and a monster, but it was ours and we were going to love paying the fifteen dollars per month installments. More than anything since, my heart rejoiced at the purchase of that old piano. Ellen had done so much for me. I was pleased as a child and would have brought it as a gift in outstretched hands, except for the fact of its heart of solid stone. We had the perspiring movers place it along the wall nearest the door (after three flights up!) because we couldn't watch them suffer anymore, and although we stayed in that apartment two years, we never dusted underneath our "instrument." We felt Christians just could not afford the luxury of having the piano movers in each time we cleaned the living room. But you will see a bit later on that Jesus used that old dust-catcher to bring His music back into my heart, and one time in particular it might have been directly responsible for the fact that you heard "Unshackled" on a certain Saturday evening in 1952.

One other important thing besides the piano was "given" during that first month after we moved out of our "whited sepulchre" and into our nice, unexciting, normal South Side apartment. And the thing that was "given" was truly given.

For several weeks before we moved, I had been in correspondence with a commercial artist who listened as she worked each day to "Visit with Genie" in her Michigan Avenue studio.

"If Jesus Christ is as exciting as you make Him sound, I'm interested," she wrote.

And during the first month on Cornell Avenue, the time came for His "giving." Her name is Alice Crossland and she came out to eat spaghetti dinner with us. But before we did that we three knelt by my studio bed in the back room where I wrote and slept and He gave her the gift of Eternal Life, at the same moment He gave *us* her friendship, which we thank God is eternal, too!

The thing that was "taken away" was also a gift as we see it now. In the Kingdom, each seeming tragedy is so closely followed by a special joy that the telling at times is a task for colors and not for words. One morning while my microphone was cut off during the playing of a long recording on a "Visit with Genie," the station manager called me into his office. I expected the promised raise and I went in thanking God ahead of time.

"I know you don't have time to sit down, Genie, because technically you're still on the air, but I have bad news. We're having to retrench on expenses. Your program is outpulling all the others, but . . ." He stopped, embarrassed.

"You mean you're cancelling the afternoon 'Visit with Genie' and my raise?" He looked so sad I smiled. "That's all right. I take God literally. He promised to take care of me. Don't feel bad about it."

"You don't quite understand, Genie. We're cancelling your work with us altogether. This is Wednesday. You'll have to wind things up by Friday of this week. Of course, we'll give you two weeks severance pay."

The poor fellow lighted a cigarette nervously. "Say, you'd better get back to your show. That record's almost ended."

Two things happened in me.

One, I remembered those little wooden toys with round bottoms my brother Joe and I had when we were kids. Mine was a clown and when I hit him, he rocked way over to one side and then he came right back up again.

I thought of him and then I thought how heartbreaking it would be to have been the poor man who had to fire me! For me this was not only a completely unusual reaction, but it warmed me inside in a strange and tender way and I felt tears on my cheeks as I hurried back to my studio to say good-bye to my loyal, loyal listeners for that day. Of course, I couldn't tell them what had happened. But I felt so near them all during those last eight or nine minutes when I adlibbed an even more affectionate than usual good-bye.

"Unshackled" was big and showy and exciting and strictly a pioneer venture, but my heart was in my informal "Visits" with the dear people I would never see, and "Unshackled" didn't help absorb the shock at all. Except to realize that He had that set and going before He allowed me to lose my other job. Neither did "right thinking" nor my courage absorb the shock. The Everlasting Arms absorbed it and lifted me up rejoicing and strangely excited about everything.

I was supposed to take the South Shore Electric out to Michigan City, Indiana, that day to interview a woman who worked in a big hospital there. She had been converted at the Pacific Garden Mission many years before and I had scheduled her story for two weeks from that date.

There was nothing to do but go right on to Michigan City after I got off the air that morning. Everything in me wanted to call Ellen and say, "Hey, St. Paul is right! I'm rejoicing even though I've just been fired!"

There was just time to make the train, though, and at the hospital in Michigan City, I met a dear little lady with pretty gray curly hair in two pink bows and a story that turned out to be one of the strongest and most loved stories which we have ever done on "Unshackled"! Her name is Hattie Matthews and even though our worlds are far apart, we are sisters in Christ. And I am always so happy when

Hattie comes slipping timidly into the big, brightly lighted "Unshackled" studio at WGN; this she still does every few months to visit her friend, Genie Price, whom she loves.

Genie Price really loves Hattie Matthews, too. When she was young and desperate, the Lord caught Hattie in His arms just before she jumped into Lake Michigan. The same arms held me that warm fall evening when I walked into our apartment just as Ellen was setting the table for dinner. I brought a big bunch of heather in a roll of green paper, and Ellen didn't even stop unwrapping it when I said:

"I've got news for you. I was fired today."

I loved the job and we needed the money but He knew all these things and it was all right with us both. Our inner climate remained the same. The heather looked lovely in a big copper urn I had salvaged from my old life and it lasted until we moved almost two years later.

"Seek ye first the Kingdom of Heaven . . ." and the burden will be light!

27

A New Un-Daily Life

It was exactly right, as the Lord knew, for me to have had a set schedule of two broadcasts daily because I had always loathed routine and insisted upon working at night simply because people with dull and regulated lives worked during the day. Since "individuality *is* all elbows," I kept the skin knocked off mine and the Lord began putting an end to my "individuality" with the regular "Visit with Genie" broadcasts. One day I actually found myself feeling cozy and glad to be one of the same people every morning on the bus. Nothing more was demanded of me than was demanded of them and I just got off and on and was glad not to have to bother about being noticed or special.

And so, from this one standpoint it was certainly all right for me to be back on "my own time" during the day again. We don't need the crutches of certain hours and certain occupations in order to bring out our "best" *if* the Holy Spirit has *remade* our weaknesses and faults into His own personality traits. He felt He could trust me with making my own disciplines by then and He was right. I wanted a schedule. And as soon as He saw He could trust me with following it, He began to cause things to intrude upon it. This was to prevent my growing inelastic and becoming as "fastened onto" my schedule as moss is limited by the rock to which it clings. The Lord wanted His child to be free because of His Father-Heart and His need of her, and so after He taught me to love scheduling things, He then taught me not to mind to have the schedule knocked off schedule.

"Unshackled" was attracting the attention of the Christian world in the Middle West and invitations for me to speak to groups of all kinds began with one or two and increased to ten or fifteen a week.

"Isn't it amazing that they want *me*? Oh, I know I'm the writer

122

of 'Unshackled' but I've been so unpleasant about Christians for so many years, I think they're wonderful to want me at all!''

Ellen reminded me about Paul and I knew it was because of what Jesus had done for me that they wanted me, but I was still so grateful and tried a very foolish and immature thing. I took four and five dates a week and still continued to interview, write, direct, and produce "Unshackled." In May, 1952, I spoke at a different Mother and Daughter Banquet *every night* in the month except Saturday and Sunday! My determination to lose weight until my body is a fit temple for the Holy Spirit, got me out of most of the eating, but in elegant restaurant after restaurant and church basement after basement, I slipped in night after night to tell the well-banqueted mothers and daughters how much Christ had done for Genie Price and her mother. I told them the very suit I wore was one Ellen had remodeled from Mother's oversupply still hanging in her closets at home. And that year they all were. Mother and I had allowed many things, including well-cut suits, to occupy the center of our lives. But now He is there, and we are using up the suits as He restores the years the cankerworm ate away. Mothers and daughters wiped their eyes and some were friends again when they left because I didn't mind telling them that now that Christ had His arms around us both, Mother and I were closer than ever before. And that we expected to love each other more and more as we each came to belong more completely to the One we had crowded out so long.

One night in a church in a nearby Illinois city, I stood behind the coatrack in the church parlor downstairs and prayed with my one arm around a mother and the other arm around her daughter. They had been strangers for a long time but they left holding hands. The mother had let the wall between them crumble. The girl said good night to me with a radiant, much prettier face, because she no longer had to carry around the weight of her double life with Mother. She had my sympathy and I wish I had known Jesus Christ could do things like that when I first started to deceive.

I might have been called Miss CTA of 1951 and 1952 because the once-elegant, would-be successful career woman who had to call

Union Club Motor Livery for a limousine to take her six blocks south to the Wrigley Building for a recording session twice a week suddenly found herself rattling around Chicago and suburbs on the once-despised elevated and subway trains, whizzing up and down the lakefront on the South Shore and I.C., packing in and falling out of streetcars and buses and loving every minute of it. Someone now and then came out of his or her own troubled world long enough to look at me as though I might be dangerous because I sat there in the crowded cars and smiled. They didn't know I was thinking about my Beloved. I wish they had known. Because they all needed to smile, and without Him there's no point nor reason for it.

My new "un-daily life" rocked merrily and busily along. Ellen's work equaled and some days was more than mine because the telephone and the mail deliveries continued to call more and more of her attention to themselves. On the days when she was swamped, I muddled happily around the house, putting up rods and cleaning paint off the windows. And in the spring we planted morning glories in two wicker ferneries some dear friends gave us. These we set on our five-by-eight front porch over which hung a little elm tree which God had planted there at just the right time enough years before so that it nodded and waved at us in 1951 and 1952.

Soon after we moved to Cornell Avenue, I spoke to a Writer's Conference sponsored by a Christian publishing house in Chicago. A lady named Charlotte Quilty came to hear me and walked quietly and forever into my heart—into Ellen's, too, as soon as they met. And one day Charlotte arrived at our house with visible proof of His promise to "add all these things." Under her arm she carried a large bolt of lovely rose-colored material, and following her up the three flights of steps came her little niece, Corine, smiling too, her brother, Donald, with a big sack of groceries and her dear friend, Florence Heller with her portable Singer in her hand. Charlotte, like me, couldn't sew, but Florence could and soon we all loved each other and laughed and praised the Lord while Don put up curtain rods and Florence sewed her fine seams. About the middle of the afternoon, Charlotte cooked the food she had brought along, Florence fitted the brand-new spread on Ellen's studio bed, Don hung the brand-new draperies. And in a day of fun and real Christian fellowship, the Lord, through dear Charlotte Quilty, had transformed our bare living room into one that looked like a home. We thank them all from our hearts for the draperies and the bedspread, but most of all we thank them for being available when He needed them to help His Cornell Avenue "charges."

Many letters came from many people; some of them were on plain paper and some on cards with orchids in the corner and Scripture verses at the bottom. Very many came with large red roses taking up most of the first page. But one came on the loveliest Chinese paper with a thin bamboo design. The note was routine—an invitation to speak at a Pioneer Girls' "something" at a church in Rockford, Illinois. And it was signed, as so many letters from Rockford, Illinois, are signed, with the name of Carlson—Mrs. Don Carlson. It so happened that I could take the date and I went. After I spoke I met Mrs. Don Carlson. But before I did I asked about the woman with the peace in her eyes and the certainty of God in the way she was about everything. "Who is that lady over there?" I asked someone.

"That's Marguerite Carlson. She and her husband and son were prisoners of the Japanese during the war. They're missionaries to the Chinese."

I wasn't surprised. I learned that night that one doesn't need to proclaim loudly that one has been through deep waters and furnaces with lots of fire in them and that one has found God to be ever-present. It's good to tell, but one doesn't have to shout, one just has to have depended upon Him as Marguerite had been forced to do the day they took her beloved husband, Don, away in a Japanese truckload of other prisoners. She was left there with her son, Bruce, and she took Bruce's little hand and walked right through her fear and her self-pity into the arms of Jesus Christ. And it shows on her face. Later on you will see how He planned to use the Don Carlsons in our lives.

It was then that almost everybody began to be Swedish. Swedish and generous and lovable and kind. And if God has a nationality, through which He "covenanted" to look after these two girls, the Swedish people could call themselves "God's chosen." This is no doubt the coincidence of the proximity of Chicago to Rockford and Minneapolis, but *we* insist upon at least a capital C if *you* insist upon the word "coincidence" in connection with the relief from near tragedy which struck us just before the New Year of 1952.

Ellen awoke one morning with violent pains in her left forefinger, and being lefthanded except when using scissors, it bothered her all day. By nightfall it was red and swollen and the inflammation showed in her hand, too. The pain increased and neither of us wanted to admit what we feared in our hearts. And even when the doctor told her the next day that it was "acute inflammatory arthritis" and added quite humbly that he could do nothing beyond giving her penicillin shots which at best were only temporary, we still tried not to talk about it and I was touched and impressed with her courage.

I took over the dishwashing and laundry entirely, also with no comment, and was careful to appear to pay no attention to the outstanding fact that she couldn't type or play the songs about Jesus we loved of an evening after dinner. No more songs about Him, no more Bach, no more music at all. Also no more coffee and the alarm set every four hours all night long to give her the kind of "test" pills the sincerely helpless doctor prescribed. We knew much arthritis is emotional in origin, and this was a temptation to spiritual depression which sharpened the awareness of the pain and the helplessness she felt because suddenly I had to do more than my share of the work.

Once I caught her standing at the kitchen sink washing dishes with one hand and I saw tears on her cheeks because of the occasional touch of hot water on her red and swollen hand.

And then God had a Swedish gentleman call our number. The kindly man of seventy years who one night had walked smiling into studio 6B where we used to do "Unshackled" and after looking us over to see if we were "as good as our product," handed me a check for one hundred dollars in support of the program. Later he sent similar offerings to the Mission itself and a warm bond of Christian friendship sprang up between this dignified gentleman and ourselves.

More than once he took needy people to a Loop department store and outfitted them top to toe. We knew he was a heavy supporter of the famous Lutheran Hour and we thanked God that Brother John had turned over his plenty to God to use as He wanted to use it. And so, when he called our house this night in January of 1952, Ellen was glad it was Brother John because although we had only seen him once for a few minutes, he had become a friend. He was fatherly and kind and Ellen was alone and in so much pain. They talked a long time about the program and about the church where I was speaking that night and then Brother John asked: "How are *you*, Ellen?"

Up to this point she had told very, very few people about her hand—just those whose prayers we valued most; and so she was surprised to hear herself reply: "Oh, I'm in a lot of pain with arthritis in my hand!"

When I walked in the front door that night, I knew something wonderful had happened.

"There's been an answer to prayer, Genie! Brother John is sending me to a Mr. Polson who has a health food store and has a combination of natural foods and vitamins which are curing arthritis. I'm going to call Mr. Polson on the telephone tomorrow!"

I am the daughter of a dentist and that means I grew up in the school of "medicine" and at that point anything *not* suggested by a practicing M.D. drew a raised eyebrow from me.

"Health foods? Doesn't that seem kind of—remote?"

"I know what you're thinking, but I believe the Lord has sent this. Brother John says Mr. Polson is a Christian and opens his shop every day with prayer and I'm sure it will work! I'm just sure of it. And another wonderful thing, Brother John is having the bills for the vitamins and stuff sent to him. He buys quantities of this food every month for people who need it but can't pay for it!"

Brother John must have slept sweetly and soundly that night. Surely he had heard the Lord's Voice and he had obeyed. Ellen went to see Mr. Polson and whether it was his prayers or his pills, or the combination of both, her hand was completely well within one month!

It has been well ever since. And it rests even more quietly in the Lord's hand now than ever before.

It was certainly all right with us that about this time so many people began to be Swedish. And they did—except for the Scotch Covenanters who, blessedly for me, came into my new life during the second year of it when one afternoon I met Dr. A. J. McFarland, Field Secretary of the Christian Amendment Movement, in the lobby of the Pacific Garden Mission Servicemen's Center. This gentle-looking, quiet-mannered man waited patiently for over an hour while I interviewed someone for "Unshackled." This is a drain on me because of the close identification with the suffering in the person's life, and I felt quiet, too, when I walked over to Dr. McFarland. He said very little except that he represented a group of people who wanted to recognize Jesus Christ in our National Constitution. Until that moment I hadn't realized that there is no mention whatever of God in the key document of our great country. I felt a strange compelling to take this man's suggestion seriously. Time after time I had gotten the red light from the Holy Spirit when certain well-meaning Christians called with absolute guidance for me to take on their TV or radio programs. Somehow this was different. Having used the high-pressure methods of the world for so many years, I was peacefully aware that "A.J." did not use them. He just told me that they wanted me to write a half-hour drama setting forth the purposes of the Christian Amendment Movement.

I prayed about it and wrote and produced it and it has been broadcast on hundreds of radio stations across the country. I began at once to write a column for their official publication and I called the column "The Way Out." As you will see later on, this must have been guided, because these "columns" came together in a ministry which reached far beyond the circulation of the little paper.

The Scotch Covenanters sing only Psalms in their churches, but they *live* the resurrection life of the Christ whom they would honor in our National Constitution. And they own forever an inner-room in my heart.

When this half-hour dramatic broadcast, "The Way Out," began to move about the country, so did I. "Unshackled" rated an entire page in *Broadcasting,* the bible of radio, and then *it* began to move about the country; and each week new stations were added as out-and-out commercial operations began to write for permission to broadcast this Gospel program without cost to the Mission. No one was more amazed than its writer, who continues to underestimate the Holy Spirit.

But "Unshackled" grew and kept growing like eternal life from "inside," as we purposely avoided the more sensational methods of promotion. I felt separated from the program's growing fame because I, of all, knew He wrote it through me. Week after week the scripts kept pouring out and life was good and creative and busy and my heart sang. People came up to me after speaking dates and asked how I got that singing way. In those days I always had a glib answer.

"We can all be this way providing we belong to Him—all the way!"

I took no credit. I felt I deserved none. But my answer was glib and immature, although it *was* true. But not of me, as I thought. What I had was in part head-knowledge of the marvelous workability of the "life hid with Christ in God." But I believed with all my heart that He did have all of me and so naturally I rattled off the answers.

Everything increased, including my salary on "Unshackled." The speaking date fees moved from five dollars and/or "thank you so much, you have blessed our hearts" to love offerings and what the letters called "suitable honorariums." And life was good and my heart sang a clear song and I couldn't imagine that *anything* could ever go wrong for me again. Each week Jimmy McGree (the potentially legendary Pacific Garden convert who played the "part" of the Skid Row drunk who broke a bottle over the hero's head in their film called "Out of the Night"), made regular pilgrimages out to our apartment to pick up the freshly written scripts and take them "indispensably" to the continuity department of WGN. Jimmy puffed up the three flights of stairs, caught us up on the Mission gossip, made an immortal observation or two about life in general, reported how many letters the show was pulling and life was good for us. It even had Jimmy McGree in it and darkness was remote and agony of soul "impossible."

I would have laughed if anyone had told me they were both about to come.

28

"How Great Is That Darkness!"

On Christmas day in 1951, we shared our home and the baked ham my family sent us with six people who, along with us, might have posed for an artist painting a picture called "Redemption." He could have placed us all at the foot of the Cross and we would have been excellent subjects. Around our table that day, singing Christmas carols at the top of our voices because we *understood* about "God and sinners being reconciled," were an ex-gambler, an ex-carnival man, an ex-alcoholic whose home was still broken up, another ex-alcoholic who is a headwaiter, an ex-small-time gangster, an ex-big-time gangster's girl friend, and Ellen and me.

Neither of us will ever forget this day. His Redemption was so real we could feel it all around us. We knew beyond the shadow of the merest doubt that "the Lord had come" and that the ground *is* very level at the foot of His Cross.

Deeper in me dwelt the Christ of manger and the Cross and the open tomb when that day ended and I dwelt more deeply in Him. And yet, after that, in the spring the darkness came. And agony of soul and mind and spirit that made me want to strip the little sticky red buds off the trees and stamp them into the still frozen earth! This was not what the saints call the "dark night of the soul," when God seems to withdraw His Presence. God's Presence haunted me, and the "footsteps followed, followed after" no matter where I ran. And I did run. And I stumbled and was bruised and I wept and then I ran some more because it was all such a surprise to me that the darkness had come at all and especially that it had come to me.

I pushed myself doggedly through one "Unshackled" script after another. I stood before hundreds of people telling them what Christ had done in my life, but night after night I forced myself to stand in pulpit after pulpit when I wanted to break and run for the nearest bar. Not because I craved a drink, but because I was so afraid of the new darkness.

And the darkness came when I was trying to turn on the Light!

The darkness came when *I was trying to turn on the Light—myself.*

And this is the way it came.

One day, when all seemed so well, as I sat writing at my desk my telephone rang and on the other end of the wire, a most interesting voice said:

"I'm not calling to ask you to save my soul, I simply want to tell you that I think 'Unshackled' is a writing masterpiece! On top of that, the production is out of this world, but that's *all* I want to talk about. I am definitely *not* interested in salvation!"

In a few days, as a result of that call, I ignorantly and glibly and excitedly led this person into—*not* a true walk with the living Christ but into a sort of subjective fascination with *my* conception of Him.

And out of this the darkness came.

Only a shadow at first, when I became intrigued with the way I talked about Him to other people . . . then a kind of thick twilight began to settle when I observed with pride the effect of my words of persuasion and even though I used the "right words" and quoted the "right Scriptures" and had the person pray what was a "more attractive" version of the publican's prayer—"God be merciful to me a sinner"—it all turned back upon me and when I saw what I had done, I threw open the door of desperation and all the darkness of Hell rushed in upon me.

But He stood in it showing me that I had "converted" not only this person, but two or three others to *my* Christian "self." They were clinging to me and therefore they had nothing to which to cling.

Sequence is not clear to me now. But it began to take ten and twelve hours to write "Unshackled" instead of five or six. The words seemed to pull themselves up to the edge of my typewriter carriage and peer at me and some of them piled up on top of each other and others slipped back down inside the machine and refused to be used at all. My voice snapped when I answered the telephone and Ellen annoyed me when she rattled things in the kitchen while she prepared our meals. The actors were slow taking cues on Saturday nights and suddenly no one seemed to understand what I wanted out of a certain line in a script, or from a particular scene. I knew what I wanted wasn't there and I was irritated that the cast didn't get it out anyway. My desk drawers stuck and my galoshes wouldn't slip over the heels of my shoes and I was so nervous I sat after dinner each night drumming the top of the table, with every cell of every fiber of every nerve center in my body crying out for a cigarette!

All at once, I began to notice the music on the neighbor's radio across the four-foot areaway outside my study and the beat of it pulled me back and back and back. I remembered old faces and instead of praying for them I longed to go back to them and shout, "I'm back! I was only kidding. I didn't mean to go away. Christ isn't real—but we are, and I love you, all of you. Will you take me back?"

Christ isn't real! *Will you take me back?*

One night I cried and stormed and shouted the more loudly when Ellen tried to remind me of the girls in the back apartment.

"If Christ *is* real and if something has *really* happened to me— if I'm converted or saved or whatever you want to call it, why do I feel like this? If I've 'seen the light'—if I'm *in* the light, why is everything so doggone dark?"

And then I cried and cried and cried.

And after the whole night I slept an hour and went to speak at an 8:00 A.M. chapel service to the staff of a Christian publishing house in the Loop. My eyes were red-rimmed and swollen but on the train going uptown, something happened. I knew I'd be sunk without Him when I faced all those Christians who admired "Unshackled" and so for my hour of need, at least, I turned my face back to His face. And miracles followed the speaking date that morning. Miracles and one very amusing incident. Even though I confessed my night-long battle, I spoke of the joy that had come in the morning on the train. And afterwards, two old sisters discussed me in the ladies lounge.

"I don't think she's saved at all, do you?"

"No, I don't. She's too happy!"

I didn't hear about this conversation until much later, after even more darkness had come and long after the uneven, hectic days had been replaced by the "peace that passeth all understanding." During these tense days in March and April, I watched dark circles under Ellen's eyes grow and she slept very little even on the nights when I didn't batter her with questions and throw scenes and shoes and books. And the day she told me she had known for three weeks that in spiritual pride I had started to run my own life again, I really jerked the reins out of His hands! My own twisting guilt turned back on her and she stood taking the blows for Him until she who had been patient and long-suffering and quiet for almost two years, stamped her foot one 5:00 A.M. and screamed:

"Don't ask *me* why you feel like this! Ask Him! If the Christian life doesn't add up, don't ask *me* why it doesn't! Ask Him! You've made me an answer-box long enough. Too long! I'm sick of it and there are about five million questions I'd like to have answered, too!"

"Well, why don't you ask *Him!*" My voice had the same old edge it had before my conversion when I was trying to knock her off her spiritual pedestal.

She opened the closet door and began putting on her coat. This had always been my trick and she had no right to use it.

"I'm *going* outside to go ask Him. Right now."

"But He's *everywhere*, don't forget. That means He's here! The catechism says so."

"I know He is, Genie. But *you're* not where I'm going and I've just got to get away from you for a while. I'm sorry. But I don't know what to say to you next. I'm at the end of my rope. I want to help you, but this time I can't. I've walked into some of the darkness you yell about, too! And I'm going over by the lake and ask Him what to do." She began to cry. "He must have something to say to me . . . about *something!*"

After I heard the front door close downstairs I fell across my bed and tried to pretend I had never been converted, had never told anyone

I had become a Christian, that I was *not* the writer of "Unshackled," that Ellen Riley was back again in childhood under that apple tree playing the piano and I was back on the Near North Side just waking up out of a mixed-up dream, and that it must be time to take Spunky for a nice long walk. I needed my head cleared and I needed to be *myself* again.

About six, when the sun had decided to shine all over for that day, I heard the front door downstairs and I knew Ellen was coming home. I counted her up the three flights of stairs through the quiet early morning in the building and then I opened the door to our apartment for her.

"Well?"

"I sat by the lake for a while."

"Did He have anything to say?"

"Oh, yes."

"What did He say?"

She hung up her coat and looked at me with the same old kindness, and then she said, not looking at me at all:

"I sat there and the waves just kept coming in. Always toward me. Never away from me. They just kept coming in . . . *toward* me. All I had to do was sit there, and let them keep coming toward me."

He shouted to *me,* too, through her from the lakeside that bright April morning, and even though I didn't want to hear, I heard.

I went to bed about ten in the morning and Ellen sat down at our big, striped oak upright and began to play softly. She had been taking a harmony class one day a week, and the new chords she was learning to form brushed back and forth across her weary, crowded mind that morning and came out in the beginnings of a haunting, simple melody that reached me where I was, behind my wall of self-pity in the back room. It was like a lovely folksong about God.

I was so tired. I was so lonely for Christ. I had formed more of a habit than I realized of praying about small things. Of "lifting up" people with unhappy faces as I passed them on the street, and of thanking Him for funny little things mentionable only to God. I

missed Jesus so much I knew He *had* to be alive and I knew He had
to be God. I knew He was there, too, in the room and waiting just
outside the self-pity, waiting for me to come back to Him.

In my subconscious depths, up to that moment, I still owned the
right to take the reins back into my own hands. I had given up the
right to myself *consciously*. Now, He dared to show me what still
lay in my *sub*conscious and because He trusted Himself *in* me, He
let the "darkness" come. But He continued to work.

I threw open both windows and fanned the door to clear the air
and up the hall went the "darkness," too.

On my knees by the bed I realized Ellen was really playing that
haunting melody. She had smoothed it out by then and it said to
Him what I needed to say.

I had no words and no tears for a long time. But after that time,
still kneeling by my bed, words came to the melody Ellen had just
composed. . . .

> Silent now I wait before Thee,
> Trembling in the silence here . . .
> Cruciform and still before Thee,
> Waiting for Your healing Tear!

His healing came as it always does. Then my tears of relief and
joy. The darkness was gone, and *He* filled our house and our hearts
and kept the telephone quiet so that we both slept until after four
that afternoon.

". . . the light of knowledge of the Glory of God was *still* in the
Face of Jesus Christ."

The "darkness" was past, and the true Light shone in a way I
hadn't been able to bear before.

29

Change

When I paid the rent on our Cornell Avenue apartment for the last month of our second year's lease, I felt suddenly and unmistakably that it was time for us to move. We had a happy relationship with our landlord and his family, but he did have a family—a charming wife and a small son and daughter—and up and down the three flights of stairs from the first floor past their apartment there had staggered a not too infrequent "lost sheep" plowing up to our apartment at odd hours for help. The most refined people, when "lost" in the bottle for several days, do not look refined, and although they were almost all sincerely coming for help, our landlord didn't understand exactly what we could do for them. To save him embarrassment, we gave our notice that we would move. The landlord had said absolutely nothing. And he may read this and be surprised, but we felt such a *deep* compelling that we had to go that neither of us could refuse it. Where would we move? Didn't we know apartments were still almost impossible to find? Especially on such short notice? Yes, we knew it, but we figured the Lord knew it, too. And so we told people we were moving and made our plans to go.

For several months we had been playing at the idea of someday living in the suburbs where we'd have more time to live like average people. We talked of building a tiny pink cement-block ranch house. Maybe even of buying a car, although neither of us could drive and neither of us wanted to learn. And, of course, we had no money. But when the days were tumbled so full of complaining, trouble-ridden people who said: "Well, here I am. I'm sad and lonely and tempted and troubled and sorry for myself. What are you two going to do about me?"—when the Saturday night broadcast seemed to come around faster each week, when the speaking dates meant more

137

and more travel, and when the people still kept calling and coming and being sorry for themselves, we thought happily and longingly of our little pink cement-block house way, way out in a suburb where it was quiet and clean and where you could open a window without having to dust within the hour, and where telephone calls were toll calls.

When we knew He wanted us to make some kind of change, when we literally felt Him breaking up our "nest" on Cornell Avenue, we both thought of the peace and quiet of the suburbs, but what we did was tell two friends who were real estate brokers on the Near North Side that we were apartment hunting back there again.

It is even dirtier Near North than in Hyde Park where Cornell Avenue is, but it is centrally located and the people who were afraid to ride trains could get to us there. We knew He needed us in the city.

We longed for the peace and quiet of the country. Any writer in her right mind longs for a few hours of uninterrupted writing time. And Ellen's main relationship with her piano by then was to look at it standing tall and silent where the movers had put it, while she sat at her extension phone and listened and listened and listened and talked a little and then listened and listened and listened.

We thought about a clean, little new house in the country. But we knew He wanted us in the heart of the city where people could get at us even more easily! We had no right to run away from them. We believed we had no rights to ourselves whatever.

"Lovest thou me?"

"Yes, Lord, we love You!"

"Then feed my sheep."

Thus we made our plans to move back to the Near North Side where the "sheep" would know our voice and where we spoke their language and where they needed the Shepherd so much. We had no idea at all where we would move, but we got all ready to go and told people we'd have a new address Near North by November first.

30

When the Lord Moves

When the Lord moves, He is not easily tracked down a printed page. And depending upon your intimacy with Him, you are going to be variously surprised and amazed at the deft strokes of His hand and the swiftness of His workings once the start was made.

As soon as He looked into our hearts and found we were willing *never* to live in the suburbs if He wanted us in the city; as soon as He saw that we would *really* be "broken bread and poured out wine" for *anyone* who didn't belong to Jesus Christ; when He saw we were *really waiting* for Him to make the next move—He made it.

And followed it with one after another, each swifter and more awesome to us than the one before. As He worked, we alternately clapped our hands with joy and stood by in silent wonder at what God will do for two people such as we, when we will only belong to Him literally.

We belonged and waited and acted according to what we could grasp of His workings.

We did nothing more.

But there was motion everywhere at once and swiftly!

An old friend of mine named Jane, one of the two real estate brokers, called us sometime during the first week in September. When Ellen heard Jane's voice she felt sure she had found an apartment for us.

"No, apartments at the rent you gals can pay are hard to find. But I've got a *little building* you could buy!"

Ellen was talking to her. I was out speaking somewhere and when I came home late that night, tired as I was, I thoroughly enjoyed the ridiculous suggestion.

Buy a house?

Jane knew I had closed Eugenia Price Productions at a loss. She knew Christian salaries did not permit large down payments on houses. Even if this required a small down payment, which it did, as down payments go, it was madness for us to think of buying a house.

"I'm not sure I want to be saddled with a house anyway," I said, feeling suddenly nervous, as one feels when the Holy Spirit is working in the deeps, and there is rebellion.

"Christians are not supposed to stack up worldly goods!"

This didn't ring true either. It was a deliberate twisting of a text, and I knew it. There was nothing resembling "stacking up" in the purchase of a house.

"All the money we have is sacrificial money, Genie." Ellen was stunned, too, but still she said: "Perhaps the Lord wants us to stop paying out rent for something that isn't going to end up belonging to Him."

"You mean if we used rent money to make monthly payments on a house of our own, the money would stay in Kingdom work. It would still be His."

"Wouldn't it? Wherever we live, He lives. We just live *with* Him."

"That's much better than having Him live with us, isn't it?" I smiled and so did she. We were catching the light He threw faster and more frequently than we did before. And there were active charges in the light we "caught" that night, because down deep inside us began to stir a real desire to *see* Jane's "little building." Maybe the Lord wanted to buy a house!

Jane came to the "Unshackled" broadcast the next night, and we talked afterwards over supper at London House. In the afternoon, September 7, 1952, we met Jane and went to look at her "little building." It was on a short North Side street called Germania Place, because the big old Germania Club stands on one corner. I remembered the street because the Red Star Inn, a famous German eating place, is on the other Clark Street corner. Otherwise no one pays much attention to Germania Place because it is only one block long, and up and down it from Clark west to LaSalle, for its entire unmajestic length stands one garage and exactly five old houses, one of them just fifteen feet wide including the lot. This "one" is very dear and typical of things right after the Chicago fire when it was built. Its freshly painted red-brick front looked clean and unlike the rest of the unpainted street as we approached it that first afternoon; and from under little high arched white eyebrows over its upstairs casement windows it kept an eye on an old "character" with a bushy gray beard snoozing on its wooden front steps. His head was propped against the quaint black iron railing which (unlike some) matched the little iron fence thrown protectively around the front lawn. The "lawn" rambled west for a good eight feet and north and south for the distance it took the wooden steps to climb up to the front door, and in it most serenely stood the Lord's answer to our suburban longing for green growing things.

For "green" things anyway, because although I am fairly sure it has not grown any for twenty years, looking to us like an exotic oriental tree of life, there swayed gracefully in the front "lawn" a tired lilac bush which had all turned to top and had forgotten it even intended to bloom.

That was outside.

And we were reasonably charmed by it.

Inside was a different thing. Different from anything we had ever seen. Dark and dingy and poorly remodeled and above our heels cracking and sticking on the ugly linoleum covered floors was the lingering sound of the weariness that was too heavy for the recently departed roomers to take along when they all moved out. A German family named Wilson owned it once and there was happiness in it then. The people who owned it that day when we saw it had meant to remodel it for their own home. But someone rented it and then subrented it instead, and the pictures on the walls and the faded silk cords tied to the switches of the glaring ceiling lights hung long and dejected and made us want to pray for the people who had so recently tried to "live" here. It was not dirty, just dreary and very empty and very shadowy with heartache that day as we walked through the long narrow Victorian front parlor through a crooked doorway to the "back parlor" and into the kitchen with falling plaster and a knock-kneed sink and down the back stairs into the "studio room" as advertised. This was a single wall of uninsulated bricks built up to a broken skylight all covering what had once been the backyard.

Downstairs in the basement was a very "roughed-in" bath, but the second floor showed possibilities of recapturing some of its old charm. We could rent the upstairs in order to make the payments, Jane said, and we talked some more and left—both of us shuddering.

What did the Lord mean? What was He saying in this? Was He saying *anything* or had we gotten way off-center?

"Christians can do that!" Ellen reminded me. "A lot of people say God is telling them to do something just because it's what they want to do."

Did we *want* to take on a remodeling job like that?

Even more insane than the idea of remodeling was the idea of a down payment! It required a six-thousand-dollar down payment. We had between us more money than we had ever had in our entire three years. But it was just about enough to move us north and pay one month's rent on a hundred-dollar apartment.

The thing we simply could not fathom was why we had gone to see the "little building" in the first place. We loved Jane, but she didn't have time to show buildings just for love's sake.

We talked of little else that Sunday evening after we went home. Already we felt "moved." The Cornell apartment was simply a place to stay until we found our new "home." It had been ours and we had loved living there. Now it was strange and we were really gone.

"We'd better look for an apartment in the classified section. After all, we do have to move now. We've given notice."

We found nothing and our thoughts flew back to Germania Place.

From a mutual shudder at the gloominess and ugliness of the "little building's" interior, we began to make tender jokes about it. Then we began to say tender things about it that were not jokes at all.

Then we began to feel tenderly toward the "little building."

Then Ellen said: "Poor little thing, it's just standing up there all alone doing the best it can! Like 'Little Toot,' the tugboat. Remember

the song about Little Toot you used to play on 'Visit with Genie'?''
And we laughed and we don't recall which one weakened first and
admitted that either we were losing our minds or the Holy Spirit was
putting a love for the "little building" *into* our hearts.

We had long ago found out that He can and does do this when
something is in His will. And judging from what followed swiftly
after, He did just that with our hearts and Little Toot.

But what about the six-thousand-dollar down payment?

I thought of my parents but remembered their indebtedness on the
new house they had built and anyway that would be "figuring an
angle."

And we wanted this to be entirely the Lord's doing. We knew
we'd be sunk otherwise. Ellen remembered that Brother John had
said we should call on him for help anytime we needed it, and
certainly the Lord had sent him. So, the next day, Ellen called him
and the biggest miracle to date outside of our redemption took place
when Brother John said:

"No, I can't let you girls *borrow* six thousand dollars! And anyway,
I think you'd made a mistake to buy an old piece of property in the
city when you could be out in the suburbs where people would leave
you alone. But the Lord told me quite a while ago to *give* you girls
a down payment on a house. I've just been biding my time, waiting
for His time to do it. I'd like to see you in the suburbs but if you
think Little Toot's the house, go ahead and sign the papers. The
Lord's check will be in the mail tomorrow. And it's *not* a loan!"

We "closed the deal" with Jane and the nice owners, in Jane's
lawyer's office on the following Thursday, September 11, 1952.
Perhaps it is the first time in history that two people have been
excited about buying a house they shuddered at the only time they
saw it before the papers were signed.

When they were signed, we hurried to 115 Germania Place and
as we stood alone with Him in the narrow, dark living room the old,
ugly mauve walls glowed with a heavenly glow when we said:

"Here it is. We give it back to You now on the first day after we
signed the papers, Lord. Thank You for giving it to us. Thank You

for taking it back now. To use exactly the way You want to use it. We know You'll handle the remodeling. And the money to pay for it. We know You'll send the right people to do it and oh, God, most of all we ask You to shine so brightly in this little house that no one can ever walk into it again without *feeling* the presence of the Living God! Bless dear Brother John, and we thank You, Father, in Jesus' Name. Amen."

"When two are gathered together in my name, there I am in the midst . . . lo, I am with you alway."

We realized His Resurrection in a new way that day because He stood there with us in Little Toot's living room.

And we knew, too, that if He hadn't died, none of this could have happened at all.

"Seek ye first the Kingdom of God . . . and all these things shall be added unto you."

31

According to His Riches

Brother John, through whom God had made our Little Toot possible, took one horrified look at the house and saw that we would need careful and *Christian* remodeling. And so he sent us posthaste to Mr. Henry Staalsen, one of Chicago's best building contractors and one of God's great saints.

We had no doubt but that Jane was correct when she kept repeating that first day that the "little building" was "fundamentally sound." But because we knew Mr. Staalsen to be not only a man of sound judgment, but one also very well acquainted with "fundamentals," we relaxed a little more when he stood with his head bowed beneath the low basement ceiling and laughed his big Norwegian laugh and assured us that Little Toot was definitely *not* "modern" but *was* "fundamentally sound!" To this great-hearted man we owe much more than a few hundred remaining dollars as I write this. He has been, along with Brother John, like a father to us in our "major" undertaking.

But with all of Mr. Staalsen's "pencil sharpening," Little Toot's "resurrection" was going to cost money. And with Philippians 4:19 tucked in our hearts, we began to seek loans for repairs. We knew the Lord had a way all planned, and we would just have to try doors until one opened. Several closed. Radio writers, particularly when sponsored by religious institutions, are not considered good risks at all. And I well remember the Saturday night of September thirteenth, when my "Unshackled" organist, Lucille Becker, dropped by Little Toot with us, heard our financial problems, took one dim view of the patched-up, shadowy little building and sighed:

"My, but you girls are brave!"

We weren't a bit brave. We were just excited and not very patient

145

as we waited to find out how He was going to handle the repairs. If we had not been so sure we were in His will, naturally it would have taken great bravery. If we had not been so sure of His character, the whole thing would have been sheer madness.

But we were sure and we went right on making plans. Two dear and favorite people of ours are a couple named Ebba and Roy Baumann. Roy is a member of the Board of Trustees of the Pacific Garden Mission and owner of a large appliance store. They picked us up one night during the middle of that week and with Brother John, we inspected Toot's decadent kitchen with the idea of Roy's masterminding it into something attractive and usable. He and Brother John measured and talked over our heads for quite a while and then Roy said he would draw plans for a kitchen that would be what his trade called "ideal." We believed him literally. And if you could see our kitchen now, you would say we should have done just that.

We were willing to do just what had to be done in order to move in and had already begun to laugh about the idea of bare, ugly floors and no light fixtures and no draperies and even considered that it might be good for a laugh if we soaked the soot out of the sagging lace curtain which hung at Toot's big front window, restarched it and hung it back up to prove that a Christian can travel first class or third class and still be happy.

"We're not even planning to remodel completely now. Or until we have the house paid for and that will be nine years!" Ellen explained, "He'll provide a way for us to be warm and it will be ours and He'll be there and that's all that matters."

Brother John smiled and said nothing.

But out in the alley while we were all standing beside his car saying good-night, he asked me to step aside for a moment. And in the light from his car, it seemed as though God smiled at me, when Brother John smiled and said:

"Now, you girls go on and have Henry Staalsen fix this little dump up! Do whatever it needs and do it now. The Lord's going to need *you* too much to have you all torn up remodeling a bit here and a bit there over the next nine years. Tell Henry to fix it up now. I'm loaning you girls the money *without* interest. Then if you get sick and can't make a payment for a few months, you won't have to worry. Just glorify the Lord in it, Genie. Just glorify the Lord.''

We dropped by to see one of my old friends that night for a few minutes and she understood, for the first time, what I had meant when two years before she called me a fool for closing my own production office.

"Did you ever know me to *save* enough money for a down payment on a house plus repairs during any year I made good money in show business?''

She had to say no.

If I had dared I would have quoted a Scripture. "My God shall supply all your need according to his riches in glory by Christ Jesus!'' I didn't quote it. I remembered how I used to feel about text flingers.

But maybe I should have because I certainly had proof that night.

32

All Colors!

Ellen made a few flying trips to the Loop with scraps of paper torn from decorating magazines and another phase of the "Miracle of Little Toot" began to appear. We are both women of definite opinions and tastes. But He was controlling the entire process to such an extent that not once did she bring home a "first choice" that turned out to be my "second choice." We agreed right down the line.

But we agreed so quickly that we were suspicious and so we packed off to Des Plaines for a rendezvous with the autumn leaves at a friend's cottage, with an extra valise filled with more decorators magazines, stacks of wallpaper samples, enthusiastic letters from various houses all of whom said they were thrilled that we had chosen to let *them* "help us plan our new home!" The big valise full of samples rattled because in it, too, were squares of asphalt tile and multicolored plastic wall tiles and Formica samples on bright little beaded chains.

Everywhere we looked we saw *color*. And day-by-day the leaves over our heads as we walked along the quiet autumn riverbank seemed determined to rival the colors we had spread out and propped up all over the big living room of the cottage.

We were children again. We had been converted and had become as little children and were playing happily in the Kingdom with the King. Every night when we went upstairs to the big front bedroom, we gathered up all our playthings and took them to bed with us and spread them all out again up there. Then in the morning, while Ellen made our coffee, I gathered them up once more and propped them up again downstairs in the living room.

We played and prayed and sat with Him in the quiet and saw Him in the colors spread out before us and heard Him above us living in

148

the dying leaves and whispering His love as they brushed our hair and cheeks on their way to the ground. I wrote well and easily and did in one week what it normally takes three to do in the city. We prayed more and often for our "people" who couldn't "get at" us out there, and in two instances He "got at" them in a way we might have blocked.

Life was so good we felt almost afraid and ashamed to take it. We knew so well about all the suffering. And we knew we didn't have our joy because we *deserved* it. And out of this we realized also that when our cup is sweet we can do nothing but drink it deeply and thank Him for giving it to us.

We promised Him one afternoon that when and if our cup was bitter, we would do the very same thing.

And He pressed nearer as we walked together through the leaves with all the color everywhere. He was very interested in the colors for our little house. Our life was all of one piece. And all His. We felt as near Him when we propped up our colors and laughed as when we knelt before Him in the silence and prayed that our families and friends and everyone in all the wide, wide world would somehow find out as we had found that His burden *is* light.

33

In Him Is Motion

The beginning of my fall speaking date schedule brought us back to Chicago on October first and our Cornell Avenue apartment was merely a place to stay, filled with memories and dust. Our hearts had leaped Near North and dwelt in a little narrow building whose dimensions sounded more like a bowling alley than a house.

Mr. Staalsen's men had knocked out the flimsy wall between the front and back parlors and wrecked and removed the old pantry and a strange and ghostly shed someone had built on what had once been the kitchen window wall; although this was all shoveled out, Little Toot showed no signs of her new look yet. She just seemed more forlorn than ever to the people who came to "admire" her with us. But they were polite and now and then someone with an eye for Near North Side property and an imagination on wings saw in it what we saw. This was most particularly true of a woman who has since become a dear friend. Her name is May Von Hagen and she owns Halco Sanitarium on North LaSalle Street, where "up-and-outer" alcoholics dry out and get physically set to try it again.

May Von Hagen loved our little house and not only gave us three lovely pieces of antique furniture for what would have been a bare living room, but offered to let us live on the third floor at Halco while the house was being finished. Moving day from Cornell Avenue had been pushed up to December first, but there was no hope of getting ourselves into Little Toot before December fifteenth at the very earliest. And so we were going to save hotel rent for two whole weeks because of May's kind invitation. Eating at Halco is an experience in itself and we were really looking forward to our stay there. The manuscript for my first book *Discoveries* had to be finished by January first, and we figured Ellen could run back and forth around

150

the corner from Halco to Little Toot while I hibernated in the third floor in the big room where AA meets to peck away at my publisher's deadline.

Two extremely important and joyful incidents need to be told here. One concerns a gift the Lord made to us of a new brother. A friend from Wheaton named Ward Oury called to ask if I would talk to a lifelong friend of his who was just about willing to admit to the end of his rope. This man was a well-known actor and announcer and had agreed somewhat reluctantly to see me.

In Chapter V of *Discoveries* is the story of how we met and talked one Saturday night after "Unshackled." Ward and his unhappy friend and I sat in London House over supper and mostly I talked. The actor with the unhappy face and the seemingly hopeless eyes listened politely. I spoke of being a slave of Jesus Christ and therefore completely free.

Sometimes he didn't even seem to be there. And then he would surprise me with a penetrating question. As we parted that night I could not have told you what he really thought or how he really reacted to what I had said about my new life.

But the next Monday, Ward Oury called to report that his friend had stopped his car by the side of the road, quite alone, and had surrendered his mixed-up life into the hands of the living Christ that same night.

This man is now one of the most radiant Christians I know. He is our Christian brother on whom we can call and depend in any Kingdom emergency! He gives himself constantly and is free because he no longer has to be concerned about his own rights. In a bit over one year's time as I write these lines, he is writing, directing and producing the "Christian Brotherhood Hour," he shares a microphone with me on the nationally syndicated radio series entitled "The Way Out," and he is my announcer and right-hand man on "Unshackled."

His name is Jack Odell and I am forever grateful that he did what he did that night of November 15, 1952, the night we dramatized Leonard Pollari's story on "Unshackled." We believe God's perfect timing was in this, too, because it brought Leonard into our lives and he took complete charge of keeping Little Toot tidy as each crew of workmen finished one chapter after another of her "resurrection" story.

The second important event which seemed to dispel the last wisp of doubt in anyone's mind that Ellen and I were simply standing by watching God work took place in a railroad station in Chicago just before I took a train for somewhere to speak.

We sat enjoying good conversation and fair coffee with Dr. Frank Mead, editor of Fleming H. Revell Company, in response to a letter he had written after having read an article about me in a magazine. We were overflowing with the miracle of Little Toot. Dr. Mead caught it at once and Ellen remembers his exact words:

"If you can write it the way you tell it, we'll publish it just as soon as you get it down on paper."

I called to Ellen over packing barrels and boxes of books a few days later.

"I think the Lord just this minute dropped the title to our story Revell wants. 'The Burden Is Light'!"

"The Burden Is Light!"

I tossed in another armload of books. "If we like it in the midst of this mess it must be right!"

And if you will notice the cover of this book you will see that it was.

From the beginning of "Unshackled" in 1950, until he went to a rival station early in 1953, Bill Oliver had been my announcer, and by moving day December 1, 1952, Bill had not only become our Christian brother, but offered to pick us up in his station wagon and follow the moving van as we made our pilgrimage back to our beloved Near North Side. Bill picked us up and, replete with my typewriter, a couple of suitcases, a ream of typing paper, some scripts, and the Thanksgiving turkey in a plastic bag, we set out for Germania Place. Ellen and the turkey got out there and Bill took the rest of the luggage, my Smith-Corona and me to Halco Sanitarium. Many loyal listeners would no doubt have raised puzzled eyebrows had they seen Bill Oliver, "Unshackled"'s warm, convincing announcer, helping Eugenia Price, "Unshackled"'s writer-producer, bag and baggage into an alcoholic sanitarium!

But the days sped by and upstairs in the AA room, the pages left the typewriter one after another and the work progressed on Little Toot. We owned our studio beds, my big desk, a gray driftwood kitchen table and two benches, a big rug we couldn't use, three bookcases, the Chippendale mirror, the two walnut chests Mother had sent, and four lamps. We owned a few sheets and pillowcases, a strange variety of towels that didn't match any of the five washcloths and box after box after box of books. Our tea towels had holes in them and our lamps were period pieces. And into the back "studio room" of Little Toot the husky, noisy movers piled our earthly possessions while John Karum, the head carpenter, aged seventy-two, hid *his* annoyance with us for moving in on top of them by daring the other workmen to complain. John was Mr. Staalsen's "man" on our job, and although he thought we were mostly "off the beam" on about every idea we had, he doggedly stood up for our rights with the other workmen. John holds a special place in our hearts and we take this opportunity to ask his forgiveness for all those extra moldings we "forced" him to put up.

The day we chose to move was really a day of movement. Because working in our narrow little abode on December first were John and his son, two tile men, three plumbers, two electricians, and a furnace man! I was trapped once behind my big desk and the bookcases piled on top of each other, and although I am not the athletic type, I remembered the Red Sea and made it to freedom and the "other side," three more packing crates away by the time one of the marble-based floor lamps Mother had given us toppled into the spot where I had been standing.

This same swift tempo had put the two people, out of all the city of Chicago whom God wanted to live with us, into our upstairs apartment. We had hoped to find a couple of business girls like ourselves who loved Him and who would make not only good tenants but good prayer partners. One after another turned it down, although it was reasonably priced and close in. And now we know why. When

Ellen called Harvey Jordan to ask him to make an estimate on our painting, Harvey asked to rent the apartment. The story of Harvey and Birdie Jordan is one of the most loved of all the "Unshackled" stories, and Harvey and Birdie are truly redeemed people. For years, in spite of the way they love each other, they drank and drank and drank. Until at the Pacific Garden Mission, one day very near the time He reached down for me in New York City, Christ touched Harvey and Birdie, and now we only have to open the door and call upstairs to have immediate proof positive that the new life in Jesus Christ is the only permanent release to the alcoholic.

We were advised to ask a much higher rental for our apartment. We had been given one thirteen-hundred-dollar estimate for the top to bottom painting of Little Toot. Both Ellen and I felt that even though "the market would take it" Christians should ask "Christian rentals." We believe Jesus intended the Sermon on the Mount for landladies, too, and so we held our rental down and it proved, of course, to be right. Since Harvey insisted upon doing his own decorating upstairs, we saved three hundred dollars more than we would have made had we raised the rent above their means.

"Seek ye first the Kingdom of God and his *righteousness* and all these things will be added unto you."

The Lord sent His tenants and He painted His house through Harvey, and we never wonder that everyone remarks about the magnificent decorating job in Little Toot. God makes a different sunset each evening, why wouldn't He blend exactly the right mellow stain for His pretty birch kitchen cabinets and the pine paneled walls in which He writes his books and "Unshackled?"

He took equal care of the less aesthetic aspects of His little building, too. The furnace men and the electricians were working in the house late one afternoon, neither group aware of what the other was doing. But with cosmic precision the furnace men ripped off the baseboard in the living room to replace it with baseboard radiators, at exactly the moment the electricians ripped out an old refrigerator motor from the back closet. And when the baseboard came loose in the living room, out marched an army of bedbugs! But, when the electrician broke the connection of the antiquated motor in the rear closet, the entire house was carefully filled with sulphur dioxide gas as the Lord did His own exterminating at no extra expense whatever!

We have never seen a crawling creature and it happened at four o'clock in the afternoon when it was time for the men to close up the house and go home anyway. Not even a working hour was lost in the process.

We told this incident one happy night after a repeat broadcast of the Billy Sunday story, when our dear friend, Ma Sunday, and the missionary Carlsons came to inspect the Miracle on Germania Place with us. Mrs. Sunday tossed her handsome head and laughed with delight at the workings of the Lord she had loved so long. Neither the Carlsons nor Ma Sunday were at all surprised at Him. And as though He hadn't kept us spinning with new things for weeks, Marguerite Carlson told us that night we could have whatever we needed to complete the furnishing of our little home from their home in Wheaton.

"He's sending us back to Hong Kong. We're leaving for sure right after Christmas. We want to be able to think of you girls using our furniture for the five years we'll be gone."

In Him *is* motion.

The next Monday's mail brought a warm, cheery note and a check for two hundred and fifty dollars from two more friends whom we had loved for a long time, and whose prayers and love and understanding are still warm and necessary around us both. The note was signed Mr. and Mrs. Stuart S. Crippen, and we only had to add a few dollars in order to carpet Little Toot's battered living room floor from wall to wall.

The carpet is soft and deep and on Saturday nights when Ellen and I can sneak home alone after "Unshackled," we love to lie on it and read the Sunday papers. Our dear Crippens' love is there especially then and He loves us through the pretty rose carpet they bought for us.

The Lord painted His house, He was repairing it, He carpeted its floor and placed furniture in its rooms and as one piece after another came from sources far apart, each one blended with the other because they had been Divinely selected.

Alice Crossland, the commercial artist who had become a Christian with us two years before on Cornell Avenue, descended upon our cypress wood kitchen table and benches with hammer and muscles flying and in no time the once sturdy-looking set was protruding from any direction around her Plymouth backed up at Little Toot's kitchen door. And very high among the gifts of love, we hold the results of her hours of back-breaking scrubbing and sanding, as she completely removed the driftwood finish and replaced it with a rich brown stain, rubbed and polished to the same brown in the tree trunks of the kitchen wallpaper we love so much!

She took upon herself also the painting of the basement front room, where we plan a prayer room after we get the furnace pipes wrapped so that the temperature does not suggest the Enemy's abode. And through her "fun with a paintbrush" the night before, as she painted and praised the Lord alone in Little Toot's basement, He also spoke to us when we needed it most. Ellen was weary with the rigors of remodeling, and I was pushing hard at the publisher's deadline on *Discoveries*. We were near tears of exhaustion as we were unpacking books one night a week before my Mother and Dad were due to arrive for a Christmas visit. It looked as though we wouldn't even be living on Germania Place. Everything was at that pre-final stage of holding up everything else. But there on the unfinished end of Al's paint job on the basement wall in big, definite letters we saw emblazoned:

"The Lord Is Risen!"

At cost, our dear friends the Baumanns had found the right electric refrigerators and stoves for both the Jordans' kitchen upstairs and ours. And just before Christmas, when we had managed to pay Roy for the Jordans' but not for ours, we received a check drawn on their tithe account to cover the balance in full.

The Father's care of Ellen was my joy in those hectic days just before we moved in and the last lingering workmen moved out. He knew I simply had to finish the manuscript. And every few days I went to a railroad station and took a short trip to speak and then back again at the book. "Unshackled" continued to demand its scripts and Saturday night came often. I was no help to her whatever. But Lucy was. Lucy, a great-hearted gal who had just a few months before been given a new life, and who showed her gratitude by becoming Ellen's right hand. By becoming Ellen's two arms, in fact, because Lucy, like me, is able, and Ellen had probably ducked under one hundred pounds during those days of perpetual motion.

Together, evening after evening, they scrubbed and waxed the asphalt tile floors, unpacked kitchenware and books and all the while Lucy was learning more about Jesus from the one who had taught me so much.

The Lord not only remodeled and painted and furnished His little house, He sent Lucy to help Ellen, and He sent me the willingness to stay away from the happy activity until *Discoveries* was in the mail.

Our dear Al Crossland surprised us with a pen and ink drawing of Little Toot which we had printed into our Christmas card for that year. On it were the words: Merry Christmas from our house to you because of Him! Even the "one way sign" on the lamp post in her drawing pointed *up*. And those who know Him recognized the symbol of the Holy Spirit on the roof of the little building. They're just pigeons and not really doves and they're everywhere, but He is in all and over all. And the day the specially made venetian blind for our kitchen arrived as another gift from our friend, May Von Hagen, we were not one bit surprised to find it matched Harvey's cabinets exactly.

By then we were catching on to the art of "expecting" and then praising. He gives when we plead, but I believe His heart longs for our expectancy.

We *expected* a deep and joyful Christmas, our first in our blessed little house. And deeper because Mother and Dad were coming to share it with us.

Muriel and Jim Bremner came bringing a suitable little tree as a gift from Brooke and Belinda, their two charming daughters, and were very "Muriel and Jim" as they tied bows and tiny candy canes all over it. Jim had gilded a pineapple in a tuna fish can and it reigned with dignity throughout the holiday on top of Marguerite Carlson's lovely china closet. And around the little tree, Mother and Dad and Ellen and I were more certain than ever that the Word had become flesh and that He still dwelt among us.

This same Christ had so changed Eugenia Price *and* her mother and father by then, that they knew a oneness together unlike any they had ever boasted about before.

There is a oneness around Him and *in* Him for everyone who wants to know it. Ellen and I had been in it for over a year by then. We were glad to share it with Mother and Dad on our first Christmas in the "little building" which was no longer shadowy and could never, never again be lonely or piled up with worry too heavy to carry away. It was just beginning to be the place where people came and left convinced that He meant what He said about His "burden" being light.

34

"Continue Ye in My Love"

No "gift shower" deliberately manipulated to "receive" can compare with the steady shower from Heaven which is still being poured into our lives. And the material "gifts" continued to blend with each other because One Person selected them!

Mother and Dad came at Christmas bearing a lovely copper and brass chafing dish without knowing we had copper hardware in our kitchen or that I had given Ellen a "moving in" present of a $5.95 copper skillet clock for the wall. I spoke in Rockford, Illinois, and Marian Carlson who entertained me in her lovely home took me to the train the next morning joyfully bearing a large and beautiful antique Swedish tray with a complete copper and brass coffee service! My organist on "Unshackled," Lucille Becker, slipped a package into Ellen's hand one night as she dropped us at home after the broadcast, and in the package was a pair of candlesticks.

Copper and brass.

People gave us copper and brass for the kitchen, wooden pieces that are right with the birch cabinets, and every piece of furniture, from May Von Hagen's antiques to the lovely whatnot from Alice Crossland's mother, could have been purposely selected to blend with the desk, bureau, chairs, and china closet loaned to us for the five years in which our dear Carlsons will be teaching their beloved Chinese in Hong Kong about Jesus. Mrs. Crossland donated six lovely pairs of nylon curtains which finished off our living room windows and completely curtained Birdie Jordan's front casements upstairs. And for the four new windows along one wall of my pine-paneled studio, Muriel Bremner remembered an elegant pair of custom-made draw draperies which rested on a closet shelf because they didn't fit the windows in her present apartment. The hand-blocked design not only blended perfectly with the color scheme of the studio, but when a skillful lady named Mrs. Niehoff cut them in half, no one was surprised at that point in the miracle doings to find they were exactly the right length and width for my row of windows.

The members of my cast furnished our little sand tile bath from brown rug to shower curtain to thick beige towels, matching carefully related beige washcloths.

Sand, beige and brown.

And after having cooked for three years in one small double-boiler, one small Pyrex stew pan, one skillet, and a pressure cooker carried over from B.C. days, Ellen had just about agreed to let me buy a set of pans on the installment plan. Then Marie Crossland and daughter arrived and left one quick evening, and I walked in sometime later to find Ellen leaping for joy that the Lord had forestalled my first possible charge account in my new life.

Stacked all over our new, sawdust-covered Formica cabinet tops was the most amazing display of very slightly used aluminum pans either of us had ever seen outside a kitchen utility department! A Crossland cousin had bought copper and we have now shared with Ellen's brother and his wife and still have more pans whose technical names we may never know.

Our electrical wiring had been done by a saintly Christian man named Ewald. And we were fresh out of words to thank the Lord when Mr. Ewald's bill came, showing all fixtures at exactly half-price. Mr. Perry Larson, who had done our beautiful plumbing, waited good-naturedly for the completion of my first series of "The Way Out" and still cares about little washers and drains in a most reassuring way.

The morning Marian Carlson put me on that train in Rockford, bearing the lovely copper and brass coffee service, it was "padded" with a banquet-size Irish linen tablecloth. We admired it and wondered what use we'd ever have for such a banquet cloth. The Lord knew Ellen's brother Bill and his Lorraine would be getting married in our living room on January 22, 1954 and the yards of lovely white linen gave the festive touch to our kitchen table and the big, white wedding cake was so beautiful and we were all so happy, no one noticed the extra yards of linen nestling on the floor.

In my purse after I was settled on the train bound for Chicago
from Rockford that morning, with the Swedish copper and the Irish
linen, I found a white envelope. In it was a check large enough to
make Mr. Staalsen's payment that short month after the move, but
most important to me then and for all the time between was the
message Marian Carlson gave me from Christ:

Ye have not chose me, but I have chosen you, and ordained
you, that ye should go and bring forth fruit, and that your fruit
should remain; that whatsoever ye shall ask of the Father in my
name, he may give it you.

Living in the Kingdom of God is living in the presence of the
King, and we feel it is the least we can do to keep things as nice
for Him as possible. The seventy-two feet of our little house run
along an alley, and within two or three days we realized that the two
shiny garbage cans we ordered from the hardware store for ourselves
and the Jordans upstairs would not begin to accommodate the bundles
and boxes and empty bottles of even one family in the buildings
nearby.

And so, having "teethed" on the Sermon on the Mount, I suggested
that we buy several big oil drums so that our neighbors would take
the hint and deposit their bundles *in*side and not *be*side "our" garbage
cans which they had already filled. May Von Hagen gave us the
name of her scavenger company for an oil drum delivery. Ellen
called and the owner, Mr. Albert Clausen, said we could mail a
check for the amount of the drums and he would have them delivered
within a few days.

On Mondays I am usually "coming home" from some railroad
station; the following Monday morning I got out of a cab on LaSalle
Street and walked the half block to our house in the pale winter sun.
And as I crossed the alley, I beheld two lovely, freshly painted black
drums with large white letters reading:

E. PRICE
115 Germania Place

For a brief moment to smile at His humor and little reminders of love, I remembered the mornings with God at the garbage cans during my "janitor era" in the first year. *Now,* He had given me oil drums with my own name on them.

Mr. Clausen had delivered the drums himself in my absence, and as he handed Ellen back my check, he said:

"We didn't know this was the Miss Price who wrote 'Unshackled,' and my wife is such a loyal listener, we want to make you a present of the oil drums. We're Christians, too!"

People in trouble came and kept coming to our little house. People in varying stages of the "new life" called and kept calling on our telephone which now had two lines.

The people who saw that I was happy when I spoke in churches and schools and hospitals began to come and call, too. And bitter, cynical, disillusioned men and women who held an arm high against any kind of organized Christianity wanted to come and talk to the woman who dared write the things that were broadcast over WGN on Saturday night on a program called "Unshackled." And particularly people began to come and to call when I went on the air myself with Jack Odell on a quarter-hour program called "The Way Out" in which Jack and I both declare we have found the "way out" of our own once messed-up, trouble-twisted, selfish lives.

People began doing this soon after we moved and are still doing · it in ever-increasing numbers.

We are *watching* all this happen.

We don't feel pressed or imposed upon or harried as long as we allow Him to do it through us. When we take one of "those days" upon ourselves, we sink. Neither of us could stand up through one day of answering difficult letters and writing scripts and listening to neurotic stories with no ending and checking train schedules and taking trains and packing and unpacking and speaking and interviewing and being interviewed and writing more scripts, casting shows and making billings and writing books and shopping for groceries and making guest appearances and pressing clothes and studying and interceding and writing more scripts and calming nervous Christians and telling actors there is no work for a month and counseling and reading galley proofs and holding auditions and writing more scripts and listening to more thirty-minute telephone tirades in the middle of dinner and explaining to well-meaning Christians who crave fellowship and big dinners that we don't seem to have enough hours in the day as things are.

"I have chosen you that you should go and bring forth fruit. . . ." And when God is good enough to give fruit in one's own country, it is a transforming thing. God is that good. In March of 1954, I, who had hated every brick in the building in my teens, was invited to hold a week of meetings in Central Church in my hometown of Charleston, West Virginia. Memories flooded in and the Glory poured down and one night, down the long aisle of the crowded church where everyone knew him, my Daddy walked and knelt at the altar. And I was there, too, when he made it forever with this Jesus Christ who had made us both whole again.

On another night of that week, my brother Joe knelt at the same altar with his wife, Millie, and left a load of crackling resentment and worry—an act which left him with a smile that is no longer merely a sign of a personality which he could always turn on and off at will.

Some who know Ellen and me think us too simple. We have found that the Holy Spirit *simplifies*. Some consider us subjective. But we are excited about our Object. And we are playing and working in the complete freedom of the Kingdom of God which makes it all right to be considered subjective or objective. We don't have to be either one at any given time anymore.

But we do have to be His.

This is not a book to prove God's supply. Certainly it is no guarantee that your experience can duplicate ours, or ours, yours. It is a book to remind you that even though you are not aware of Jesus Christ now, He is aware of you, and is seeking you as He sought me for all those other years.

This is not a book about "one way" to get a house. Little Toot may burn to the ground.

It is a book about the life by miracle. The miracle of *redemption*. The life He meant us all to live when He finished His work on the

Cross and went to sit down at the right hand of the Father. Ellen and I have no corner on the market of "abundant life." We have merely been willing to let Him prove His redemption in us.

At first I did not understand anything about what was meant by the finished work of Jesus Christ. I understand very little of it now, but I have taken it for my own. I have found living here in Little Toot—just east of the West Side Skid Row and just west of the Gold Coast—that in Him we become as one.

And complete.

Mink coats and sale tweeds and grease-soaked lumber jackets pass our little house. All these stood at the foot of the Cross and jeered as He was making possible their freedom from the ghastly contradiction of sin.

All these stood at the foot of His Cross and we stood there with them.

You were there.

Ellen was there and so was I.

Mink coats and bargain tweeds and grease-soaked jackets are all welcome in our little house because the ground at the foot of the Cross *is* level, and the alcoholic and the overworked office girl are as dear to God as the widow in her furs. All are stooped beneath their loads of self-pity. All have been set free on the Cross of Christ. All can take this free gift at any moment they choose to take it.

We can assure them of this because we took ours.

And we are free. Free and resting in the *absolute* of the Cross. Not as a symbol, as a literal resting place.

"There is a rest unto the people of God" because when Jesus had, by Himself, purged our sins, He sat down on the right hand of God—and when we believe this, we can begin at once to rest with Him.

And to live lightly in the depths of God.

On this earth, in the century which is called The Age of Anxiety, those who have been converted and have become as little children can rest as the wild stream rushes by, because they sit with Him in heavenly places and no longer need to fight that which rushes by.

They can move with it and not mind the corners wearing away. He has done a completed work and there *is* a rest.

"Except ye be converted . . ."—from the jerky struggle to the rhythm of God—from the stiff arm and the clenched fist to the opened arms and the emptied hands—from the love of self to the love of Christ—from the haughty look to the hungry heart: "Except ye be converted and become as little children . . ."

It is your loss.

And His wounds cry out to yours.

". . . they could not enter in because of unbelief."

Ellen and I have "entered in" simply because we have believed as best we can, and have in some measure taken Jesus Christ at His word. And He said:

> Come unto me, all ye that labour and are heavy laden, and I will give you rest. Take my yoke upon you, and learn of me; for I am meek and lowly in heart: and ye shall find rest unto your souls. For my yoke is easy . . . and my burden is light.

Jesus Christ meant every word He said. And because He said it, we tried it and found to our great, glad delight that He had said it because it is true.

"Come unto me. . . ."

We did.

And found the burden to be light.

35

From the Perspective
of Twenty-seven Years

In the year 1954 when I finished writing *The Burden Is Light* I had reached my thirty-seventh birthday. As I add this chapter, I am sixty-five and closer to sixty-six. In that interim, *Burden* has not only continued to be read, but for twenty-seven years, I have seldom opened my mail without at least one letter from a reader who had just found the book. Many of these letters contain a full page of questions—questions which range from a sincere desire to know about my family, about Ellen, the little house on Germania Place— the state of my faith today.

And so, I am grateful to The Dial Press for the unusual opportunity of writing these additional pages from the perspective of twenty-seven years. Few authors are so fortunate.

First, if it's important—and to many it seems to be—*The Burden Is Light* was not my first published book. It was my second. Some time ago I was asked also to revise the first one, *Discoveries,* of which I wrote in these pages. *Burden* is number two of a now rather long list of twenty-nine published titles, each molded by my continuing confidence in Jesus Christ.

Now to the house on Germania Place. Little Toot is no more. Because not many in the neighborhood bothered to care for or to restore the once-gracious houses—large or small—the developers, as developers are wont to do, took us over. In 1959 and 1960, as I recall, I began writing my long book, *Beloved World,* with buildings crumbling all around me—the wrecker's ball crashing again and again into houses which had once been the proud addresses of people who had wept and loved and laughed inside their thick, sheltering walls. I well remember wanting to weep each time I walked to my

office window on the second floor of the Germania Place house (I
had by then taken over the entire two floors) because each time I
looked out, a new scar had appeared—another once comfortable
room—blue or green or yellow—stood naked and exposed. I'm rather
proud of having finished *Beloved World* at all. The din was deafening,
the dust-thick air hard to breathe, still I hadn't agreed to give up
Little Toot. Of course, I knew I had no choice ultimately but to sell
it, not at a "fair market price," but at whatever my attorney could
squeeze out of the powers that be. And so, one day I moved away
from Germania Place and set about restoring another old house on
Wrightwood Avenue. I never drove back to see the gaping hole
where the little house with the white eyebrows had stood so bravely
for so many years. Carl Sandburg Village stands there now, sprawled
over the entire block. So, don't drive around looking, as hundreds
of readers have evidently done. You won't find Toot, or the lilac
tree in its postage-stamp front yard, except in the pages of this book.

Before the little house fell, in fact, soon after Ellen's marriage (to
one of my longtime B.C. friends, Charles Urquhart), Rosalind Rinker
came to share my ever-burgeoning speaking schedule for about three
or four good years. Until her schedule outgrew mine. I had already
begun to curtail my own appearances since I'd never had a single
aspiration to become a speaker. None whatever. And more and more
strongly, I was drawn only to writing books. The speaking engagements,
due to the radio programs "Unshackled" and "The Way Out," along
with the lengthening list of published books, mushroomed. In those
new, eager, first years of my Christian life, I interpreted every request
from an organization hard up for a speaker as a direct request from
God Himself. Many were, I'm sure. But my books began to be
tossed off too rapidly. They sold more every year, but even though
I believed all they contained, some were carelessly done. Gradually,
God got through to me that I was merely (very) human, that I was
not an absolute necessity to the advancement of His Kingdom and
that He had every right to expect me to do *well* that which I agreed
to do. The only solution appeared to be to begin to agree to do less
and less and improve the quality of what I did. Any book is more

readable if written in thoughtful silence at a desk than if tossed off between planes or (as in those now-almost-vanished days) on a train heading somewhere.

Little by little, I began to be selective. I resigned first of all from the writing and direction of "Unshackled" and "The Way Out." Rather enjoying my stiffening spine, I also began to refuse to commit myself to a speaking schedule more than a year in advance, then six months, then three. Then, it began to dawn on me that God would still love me if I spoke only a few times a year. And so, about the time I began to live more deeply and sanely and to reach more realistically for balance, God made it possible for me to write all day almost every day *and* for my longtime friend, Joyce Blackburn, to share the Wrightwood Avenue house with me.

His timing is always right, because Joyce had also begun to write the first of her now-long list of excellent books for children. Life was even more centered down in Jesus Christ, but it was also a new beginning for us both. Joyce Blackburn, among the first to have learned of my conversion all those years ago, had gone on being in my mind at least, my most perceptive friend. The one person whom I felt knew exactly *where I was* with God. The one person who neither expected too much nor too little of me—not at the outset, not today. She is still my best friend and we have shared our writing and learning experience for twenty-one years. We live on what was an "innocent little coastal island" until the developers caught up with us again, and although we have both come by very different routes, God has brought us rather amazingly to the same place in Him.

I'm sure I will always write books about what God is teaching me. Books called in the publishing business "nonfiction religious." I much prefer them to be called books about living, because after a quarter of a century as His follower, I am even more convinced that no one can *adequately* cope with life alone, separated from God.

I am in my sixties as I write this, an age I've always believed should be the very best of all. I believe I have learned much about understanding in the past years, but I haven't yet (and probably never will) understand why a woman lies about her age. Because she's unprepared, I suppose. Well, I doubt that I'm actually prepared to grow old, but in Christ I have come to long, not only for righteousness, but for wisdom. And for more balance. The decade of my fifties was—without doubt—the most meaningful, the most creative, the most alive ten years of my life. I have become wiser than to take for granted that this good period will last until Joyce and I are (according to present plans) buried under a leaning live oak in Christ Churchyard on St. Simons Island, Georgia. No one is immune to tragedy or failure or change. Neither God nor the Constitution guarantees what man calls happiness. Little Toot became a pile of rubble in the hole that was once our nice, clean basement; the developers could so change the quality of life on St. Simons Island that we might have to leave here, too. Yet God remains God when our cups are running over, as now, or when they are only half full.

Like most sixty-year-olds, I'm stiff when I first get up in the morning, I wear glasses, and I tire more quickly than when the first chapters of this book were written—of course. But I want it known that—oddball or not—this woman is looking forward to her seventies. Most of our mistakes should have been made by then—made and learned from, if we are alert at all—and at least a measure of wisdom should have come. Before my conversion to Jesus Christ, I held only one strong philosophical concept—that nothing is permanent but change. I still hold that concept, but lightly and with hope now, because I've added to it. I now know that nothing is permanent but change *and* Jesus Christ.

Only yesterday, twenty-seven years after *The Burden Is Light* was published, a dear lady wrote to commiserate with me that the Germania Place house fell to the wrecker's ball and that Ellen had married and left me alone. I thank her for her offer of sympathy, but once and for all, let me make it clear that God was in both events. He understands the permanency and value of change, too. I was too pleased with all the circumstances of Ellen's marriage to my beloved friend, Charles Urquhart, to be anything but glad. Through having read *The Burden Is Light* and from having sat in on Ellen's Bible classes in our living

room at Little Toot, Charlie met Christ and the good years they
shared were my joy, too. Now that Charlie is dead, Ellen, as a
widow, is, as always, giving Christ a chance to be His best self in
her and through her. She is brave and strong and full of hope. Her
husband was a hard man to lose—one of the most talented and lovable
and amusing men on earth—but because he had for years been cap-
tivated by the prospect of our "being caught up in the air" one day,
we know Charlie will be on hand when we *arrive*.

My beloved father and brother are gone, too, and Mother no longer
lives in her stone house on the hilltop. I have written at length about
that heartbreak in other books. But because of Mother's cheerful and
loving neighbors, Mary Jane and Nancy Goshorn, the still-courageous
woman who is my mother lives more "on a hilltop" than ever before.
She is still wise and gay and her beautiful speaking voice sounds as
young and encouraging as ever when I pick up the telephone to dial
her long distance.

Many other persons mentioned in the original edition of *Burden*
are gone from this earth too, now, but they are not dead, because
"Whosoever liveth and believeth in [Christ] shall never die." I find
I believe that more firmly than ever.

If you have read the first version of *The Burden Is Light* you may
miss small sections toward the end of the book in this revised edition.
I asked to write this added chapter and so some of the old version
had to be cut to make room for it. A few names are missing, but
my memories of them are not.

Now to my main reason for wanting to add this chapter from the
perspective of twenty-seven years. Over and over, in spite of the
twenty-eight other books of mine still in print, I am asked: "Do you
still feel the same about Jesus Christ?" Yes. Only more quietly and
far more deeply. Before I began this chapter, I reread *Burden* for
the first time in more than eighteen years. I cried a little. I laughed.
I lived through incidents, both sad and funny, which had entirely
gone from my mind in the interim. I read what the young Christian,
Genie Price, had written both about herself and about Jesus Christ
and along with some quite understandable horror at the youthful

glibness and bald, sweeping statements, I found myself helped by what she had written. In one way—because His goal for all of us is maturity—my reactions edged in places toward outright embarrassment at what I had written, but I changed none of those places. The first thirty-four chapters of this book are not my story now in the year 1982. They are my story twenty-seven years ago, just five years after He apprehended me in my darkness.

One such seemingly sweeping phrase was: "For the first time in my life I knew I was free!" That I now know that He goes on year after year *freeing* us still more in no way alters the truth of what I knew then. I am *being* freed daily and the years have shown me the eternal value of the continuing process. In other instances where I appeared to be always "dying to myself" or constantly "surrendering the right to myself," I realize twenty-seven years later that, somewhere along the line, I've found a wider truth. I don't recall exactly *when* the shift took place (thank heaven, I haven't dwelt much on my own spirituality or lack of it) but a shift did occur. *Today, I see the almost unbelievable freedom of looking past my own feeble surrendering to His surrender to us all on the Cross!* Rather than flailing myself into a state of what I once labeled a total commitment to Jesus Christ, I have somehow learned the larger glory, the wider freedom, the deeper peace of concentrating upon *Christ's total commitment to each one of us*.

Yet, I disagree basically with nothing of what I wrote in these pages so long ago. You see, Ellen introduced me to Jesus Christ Himself, not to some marginal issue *about* Him. For more than a decade, my luggage and I banged around from one church to another, from one organization to another—many of them incompatible on numerous marginal issues. I mainly escaped religious controversy in my little talks and with my books since, because I've stayed on Center by Grace, straying to no issue other than the altogether discoverable nature of Jesus Christ Himself. My belief in the absolute necessity of knowing something of what God is really like, of His intentions toward us—toward the whole human race—is down in the pages of what I consider my most important nonfiction work: *What*

Is God Like? The thread of that book winds through everything I write because it is my only dogma. Once we know His nature (what knowledge of it we can contain), we will have faith—not by self effort, but because we have learned that God did reveal Himself in Jesus of Nazareth, and because He generates faith. There are still many biblical passages which I simply do not understand, but I have gained definite insight on the one which declares that Jesus Christ *is* the Author of our faith. I have faith in Jesus Christ, not because of my fidelity—*Because of His.*

I was especially warmed by an interesting letter which came a few years ago from a straightforward, fun-sounding young woman who, with a friend, had been discussing me and their reactions to me ten years after they had each read *The Burden Is Light* for the first time as college students. "We were being very honest about our opinions of you after we had spent ten years growing in the Lord and after we'd read most of your other books. Do you know what we decided? Very simple. That Genie Price still loves Jesus."

Absolutely nothing anyone could say about me could please me more.

On the island where I live, I've learned an invaluable lesson which I could never have learned had I continued the hectic travel schedule of the first few years. I've learned how to live in *community*. I'm not only involved day in and day out with the sorrows and joys of the island's people, I'm also involved in preserving its history and its natural resources and beauty. As a packing, unpacking, panting, self-styled "ambassador," I had no time to keep my mind alert to the changing history of the years through which I was living. There was simply no time to read enough, to listen to opinions other than my own. There was little time to *think*. To *learn*. Certainly no time to learn to love in diversity. It's far easier, you know, to hear someone out in a short few minutes, toss off a few quick phrases by way of "answer," repack the suitcase and escape before the unintentional glibness backfired. Some of my old friends prophesied that once I moved to a tiny coastal island, I'd climb into an Ivory Tower and become a "literary recluse." One woman wrote: "How do you dare put a padlock on your high gate and still call yourself a Christian? I read your book, *The Burden Is Light.* You didn't feel you had a right to yourself in those days. I'm utterly disillusioned that I couldn't get through that locked gate to spend even five minutes with you!''

Well, this seems a good time to tell you about another important thing God has managed to teach me in these twenty-seven years: the somewhat difficult art of being willing to be misunderstood. I write rather widely read and extremely hard-to-research novels about the people and the history of the region where I now live. The latest one used up three years of working time. I live in a resort area where three of the novels were laid. My past-middle-aged brain simply could not keep all the complex historical research straight if I stopped to spend "five minutes" with the dozen or more carefree, vacationing tourists who drive past my PRIVATE ROAD sign every day. I wish I could. I'm anything but a recluse. But I am only one person. And so, I'm more than grateful that He has let me in on the secret of being willing to be misunderstood.

I am also asked, "Do you pray as much as you did then?" Yes. More. I've caught on, I think, to something of what St. Paul meant when he wrote that we were to "pray without ceasing." My devotional times are not as "scheduled" as they once were, but then I was knocking myself out trying to be a "good and faithful servant." You see, I've learned that He meant it when He said that He would no longer call His disciples servants, but *friends.* I have a very simple goal now: To be God's friend.

I no longer panic at dry or so-called dark periods. Through my dear Anna B. Mow, I learned long ago that if those times didn't come, we wouldn't be normal. How we feel—how I *feel* "spiritually"—seems less and less relevant. What matters is that God is *constant.* He is the *only* constant anywhere in the world.

At lunch today, before I began this added chapter, Joyce Blackburn asked one of her typically provocative questions: "Does it seem, after all this time, as though you've always belonged to God? Can you remember what it was like not to belong to Him? Is the dividing line between your two lives still so distinct?''

The dividing line is still there. I have not forgotten what it was like to live a roofed-in life. Horizons, thank God, are still falling down for me. I strongly glimpse now and then, not only the limitlessness of God—but also the limitlessness of His life lived in us while we are still on this earth. People who do not know God live under a very low roof of self-effort and fear.

Joyce pursued her questioning: "*How* does it still seem different? What, looking back, was/is the big difference in the daily routine between life with and life without Him?"

Having become a Christian when she was quite young, her question was valid.

I answered something like this: "Life isn't all up to me anymore. Someone is always there, listening, answering, being with me in the silence." And then I laughed. "You live in the same house with me. You, of all people, know that the fact that He is always there accounts for what balance I have! I never thought I'd turn out to be a remotely balanced person. But then, before I knew Him I didn't think God could really be the way He is, either."

The irrevocable fact that God *was* in Jesus Christ is still and will always be a great stretching amazement to me. And that fact *is* my balance and my peace.

Eugenia Price
St. Simons Island, Georgia
January 1982